Praise for the First Edition

From military spouses:

"Must-read for military spouses! As a new military spouse, I had been struggling (like many) with an almost hopeless feeling when it came to pursuing my dreams. In my particular case—Southern Alabama is not the place an aspiring actress wants to be stuck! However, after reading *Help! I'm a Military Spouse,* my spirit was uplifted and I realized that there are *soooo* many ways to pursue my goals—no matter where the Army sent us! With my renewed drive and new insight, I was able to do some networking and get myself into a NYC acting class, as well as land a *principal* role in a local movie. The book is funny, inspirational, and shows you that there is a way! Since I've read *Help! I'm a Military Spouse,* great things have been happening for me. Go out and get this book now!"

—Nikki C. Thomas, Ft. Rucker, AL

"Even with a lifetime with the military—Army brat, Army nurse, retired veteran, Army wife of twenty-eight years (still counting), and now Army mom with a son serving in Afghanistan—I had this book sit on my shelf for several weeks before I opened it, because for some reason I couldn't get past the title. Once I turned past the title page, I found the book to be one the best on the market today for military spouses because it is full of possibilities for this lifestyle, with resources, ideas, stories of other military spouses who have made this lifestyle work for them. I have turned down pages, underlined key points, and made notes in the margins and a list of references to share with others. This book is easy to read, practical, and encouraging, and more importantly, the authors back up their points with research and shared stories of other military spouses who have been able to use the keys of happiness and make the most of this challenging yet enriching lifestyle."

—Roz Riley

"Holly and Kathie's book is full of 'you *can* do it' stories from front cover to back. Not only do they have lots of stories of others that have been successful, they have included practical (and fun) exercises in the book to help you on your way. I especially appreciate the message of balance and establishing your priorities. Holly and Kathie have written a great book to help you see everything as an opportunity and discover your purpose in life. This is a must-read for all military spouses or anyone wanting to make big changes in their life. Life is an adventure . . . live it!"

—Phyllis Ward, Ft. Leonard Wood, MO

"A must-have book! As a military spouse of nine years, I'm so happy to see a book like this come out. I have volunteered and worked for many Marine Corps programs, and I hear over and over again spouses complain about their circumstances and how life is on hold until the next duty station or until the Marine leaves the service. This book helps you to not only identify your goals with practical steps, but how to go about achieving them in this military life. Holly and Kathie provide an abundance of resources—Web sites, books, magazines, and inspiring testimonials of successful military spouses. No matter how long you have been with the military, this book is a must-have! An excellent read with easy steps to follow and loaded with helpful advice."

—Lori Cleymans, Iwakuni, Japan

"An excellent tool for military spouses! I personally know Holly Scherer and can truly say she is the ultimate military spouse goddess. She served as my role model when I was a newlywed military spouse many years ago. When I first married, I didn't like what I saw for my 'military spouse' future. I was an Army brat but it's one thing to be a child of a military member [and another to be] married to one. I had a career before I married and had to give it up in order to move along in my husband's career. I thought that once you marry into the military, you become a second-class citizen and walk ten steps behind your husband. I also believed the only career you could have being married to the military was either a nurse or teacher because there was always a need for those positions and they were transferable. I found out through Holly's wisdom, expertise, and love that that is absolutely not true. There are so many opportunities, volunteer or paid, or ones you create yourself that are out there for us. Spouses do have choices, and Holly ever so sweetly guided me in the right direction. And now her book she has co-authored gives all of us the tools we need to survive and thrive."

—E. Feigenbaum, MO

"Military spouses *need* this book! I attended the workshop Holly and Kathie put on here in Japan. It was the best and most useful workshop I have attended.

This book is based on that workshop and its information *plus* more resources, shared experiences, and other insights I was thrilled to read! I read the book from cover to cover in two days (which is quite a task with four kids and a part-time job!). I believe that every command should present this book to its service members' wives when they marry, as well as offer it through Family Team Building Offices worldwide!"

—S. EALY, "DOMESTIC GODDESS," IWAKUNI, JAPAN

"In the ten years I've known Holly and Kathie and attended their workshops, there are no two women who have offered more practical tips for self-growth that are actually doable for me as a military spouse. Spoken from the heart and from their own trials, this book will speak to everyone who reads it and is in pursuit of their dreams."

—CATHY STERLING, ARMY SPOUSE

"There has never before been a book like this for military spouses. Fifty years ago as an Army bride, my husband presented me with a copy of a book called *The Army Wife*. It was full of such intimidating, impossible rules that I nearly hit him with it. Now comes *Help! I'm a Military Spouse* crammed full of help, encouragement, and practical tips. Just a glance at a few of the hundreds of headings includes 'Start your Heart's Desire File,' 'Get Help for Your Dreams,' and 'Ask for Help, Offer Help, Accept Help in These Challenging Times.' All of these tell you that here is a chance to stretch out and reach for a life that is uniquely your own while still living up to the challenges of a military life. Holly and Kathie, just one question. Where were you fifty years ago, when I needed you?"

—DOROTHY J. WILHELM, MILITARY WIFE, WIDOW,
AND MOTHER, TACOMA, WA

"This book is a must-have for all my friends who have a spouse deploying and for any new spouse I come in contact with."

—CONNIE FULLERTON, ARMY SPOUSE

"*Hoo-ah!* Or, as we say in the Coast Guard, Bravo Zulu for a great book!"

— ELAINE WILHELM-HASS, COAST GUARD SPOUSE

From other authors:

"This book is based on the workshops that Hightower and Scherer give to military spouses. I attended one of their workshops and it was great, but the book is even better. Like the workshop, it's giving me step-by-step instructions on how to make my life more exactly what I want it to be. I may not have much control over my husband's career and where it takes us, but this book reminds me that I still control the rest of my life. And since it's a book, I can refer back to it again and again. It's also filled with resources, lists of other helpful books, and Web sites."

—KRISTIN HENDERSON, NAVY SPOUSE AND AUTHOR OF *WHILE THEY WERE AT WAR*,

WWW.KRISTINHENDERSON.COM

"The definitive self-help book for military spouses! Authors Kathie Hightower and Holly Scherer have crafted a military family resource book that comes at a time when this kind of self-help literature is greatly needed. Their [first edition], *Help! I'm a Military Spouse: I Want a Life Too!* is the best book of its kind on the market today. It takes on real concerns and issues that face modern military families. Although this book deals mainly with issues related to female spouses (Only 6 percent of military spouses are male) I think some of the information contained could apply to both genders. This book is an upbeat, proactive approach to life. This is a MWSA 5-star-rated book! It is a must-buy for all military families! This is best book of its genre—period!"

—BILL MCDONALD, PRESIDENT OF THE MWSA (MILITARY WRITERS SOCIETY OF AMERICA),

WWW.MILITARYWRITERS.COM

"This book is a welcome and long-needed addition to the resources available to military spouses. *Help! I'm a Military Spouse: I Want a Life Too!* recognizes that many military spouses want and deserve the chance to pursue their own personal and professional goals and gives them the tools to do it. Military life necessarily involves sacrifice and comprise, but Kathie and Holly show us that, with a little ingenuity and determination, it need not be an obstacle to having a full and meaningful life on every level."

—JESSICA REDMOND, ARMY SPOUSE AND AUTHOR OF *A YEAR OF ABSENCE*,

WWW.SURVIVINGDEPLOYMENT.COM

"Hightower and Scherer have crafted a fine tool for military spouses that will help people make their dreams come true! This great resource is full of practical advice as well as real-world examples that will empower spouses to have a life of their own while supporting their partners in the military lifestyle. This book belongs on the shelf of every military family who wants to get more out of their new life!"

—ELLIE KAY, AIR FORCE SPOUSE, INTERNATIONAL SPEAKER, MEDIA PERSONALITY,

AND BEST-SELLING AUTHOR OF EIGHT BOOKS INCLUDING THE GOLD MEDALLION

BOOK AWARD FINALIST, *HEROES AT HOME*, WWW.ELLIEKAY.COM

"Help! I'm a Military Spouse will help you rediscover dreams and talents, and even create a few new ones. Most important, it teaches that your dreams are just as important as your husband's, and it trains you to start thinking that way. It's not about rebelling against military life; it's about taking advantage of military life and using some creativity to fulfill your own dreams. In essence, the authors have finally articulated the lessons of experienced military wives in a way that brings peace of mind. What took me seven years as a military wife to learn, Kathie and Holly explain in concise and very funny chapters full of wonderful anecdotes."

—MEREDITH LEYVA, NAVY SPOUSE, FOUNDER OF CINCHOUSE.COM,

AND AUTHOR OF *MARRIED TO THE MILITARY*

"What a treasure trove of cutting edge information, soul satisfying comfort, and inspiring stories. Kathie and Holly have used their considerable life experience and amazing research to design a basketful of tools perfectly tailored to the challenges of military life."

—JENNIFER LOUDEN, CREATOR OF WWW.COMFORTQUEEN.COM AND AUTHOR OF

COMFORT SECRETS FOR BUSY WOMEN

"I love this book! Kathie and Holly have created a resource for all women that will make you laugh, cry, and most of all, know that you are not alone. Even though the book is focused on military spouses, it is filled with creative ideas and heartfelt advice that will touch everyone who reads it. I marked at least twenty pages to use in my own life! Thank you, Kathie and Holly, for helping us all find our way in this oft-confusing world."

—BARBARA GLANZ, AUTHOR OF *CARE PACKAGES FOR THE HOME* AND *BALANCING ACTS,*

WWW.BARBARAGLANZ.COM

"Reading this book is like having a heart-to-heart talk with your best friend. In it, you'll find wisdom, support, humor and understanding. Accomplished authors Hightower and Scherer are proof that it's possible to enjoy all the rich adventures of military life and to follow your own dreams, too."

—SUSAN WIGGS, AUTHOR OF *OCEANS BETWEEN US,* A *NEW YORK TIMES* BESTSELLING NOVEL

ABOUT A NAVY SPOUSE, WWW.SUSANWIGGS.COM.

"Military spouses have unique challenges of their own and this book shows you how to handle them with dignity, class, enjoyment, elegance and panache."

—MARK VICTOR HANSEN, CO-CREATOR OF THE NO. 1 *NEW YORK TIMES* BEST-SELLING SERIES,

CHICKEN SOUP FOR THE SOUL, AND CO-AUTHOR, *THE ONE MINUTE MILLIONAIRE*

What Military Spouses Say about the Workshop on Which This Book Is Based

"Wunderbar! I have gained worthwhile and valuable information on how to turn my dreams into reality. I wish I had a seminar like this to attend fifteen years ago."

—GWENDOLYN A. WILLIAMS

"I would tell other spouses this about your workshop: For anyone who is depressed, down, missing their spouse, it's for them. For anyone not sure of what direction in life to take—career, hobbies, crafts, etc.—it's for them. It's a wake-up call. It lets you know you can do anything you desire and points out military spouses who have."

—FELICIA STREETER

"This was the best thing that happened to me in Germany!"

—ALICKA AMPRY-SAMUEL

"The two of you make a good combo— mother and military/career woman. You are able to relate to the entire audience."

—KENDRA COILE

"Very motivating! Makes you not want to be a couch potato."

—BARBARA CONNORS

"You both make a great team. Thanks for making my life less stressful."

—BLANCA HOWES

"All around awesome! You ladies rock! Wonderful mix of serious(ness) and humor!"

—BRENNA LIMBRICK

"This workshop shows you that being a military spouse provides new opportunities and different ones— it opens doors, not closes them!"

—MELISSA ENDECOTT

"This would have saved me a year of crying at Parris Island."

—SUSAN M.

Help!

I'm a Military Spouse— I Get a Life Too!

Related Titles from Potomac Books

Help!

I'm a Military Spouse—
I Get a Life Too!

How to Craft a Life for You
As You Move with the Military

Second Edition

Kathie Hightower & Holly Scherer

Potomac Books, Inc.
Washington, D.C.

Library of Congress Cataloging-in-Publication Data

Hightower, Kathie, 1953-
  Help! I'm a military spouse! I Get a life too! : how to craft a life for you as you move with the military / Kathie Hightower and Holly Scherer. — 2nd ed.
     p. cm.
  Includes index.
  ISBN-13: 978-1-59797-067-9 (pbk. : alk. paper)
  ISBN-10: 1-59797-067-0 (pbk. : alk. paper)
  1. Military spouses—United States—Conduct of life. I. Scherer, Holly, 1956- II. Title.
  UB403.H54 2007
  355.1'20973—dc22

                                    2006027337
ISBN-10: 1-59797-067-0
ISBN-13: 978-1-59797-067-9

Printed in the United States of America on acid-free paper that meets the American National Standards Institute Z39-48 Standard.

Potomac Books, Inc.
22841 Quicksilver Drive
Dulles, Virginia 20166

Second Edition

10 9 8 7 6 5 4 3 2

Dedication

To Jack, for your endless support and encouragement to go for my dreams. For always believing in me and understanding my desire to help others. You are the most honorable man I have ever met—I am proud to be your wife!

To my twins Helen and Jack for your belief in my work. I'm so lucky to be your mother. And in memory of my mother. My admiration for her is never ending.

—HOLLY

To Greg, for your never-ending patience with my many ideas (even if you do say "Oh, no" every time I start a conversation with "Greg, I've been thinking . . . "). My life would be pretty dull without your sense of humor and fun, and I can't imagine having to live without your great cooking.

My short answer to "How to be happy being married to the military" is to marry a man like Greg!

And in memory of my Mom who was one of the main copy editors on the first edition of this book. I just wish she could have seen the published book after all these years of me talking about it.

—KATHIE

Contents

Chapter 8: How Can I Pursue a Career While I'm Married to the Military?

Chapter 9: Wouldn't It Be Easier to Have My Own Business?

Chapter 10: To Volunteer or Not to Volunteer

Chapter 11: Try These Effective and Fun Goal Achieving Techniques

Preface

Why We Wrote This Book

We have some military spouse friends who just don't see the need for this book. "I don't get it," one friend said, "I've always loved this life, from day one." She's one woman who married into the military with her own deep sense of self already firmly in place and with a personal life plan that meshed well with military life. Obviously this book isn't for her. It's for those of us who struggle to figure out who we are and how we can make this military life work for us.

Don't get us wrong. We love our husbands, we are super proud of their service and support that service. And still we struggled with how we fit in—how we could make this lifestyle work for us too.

Many of us as military spouses feel that we've had to give up our own dreams as we follow our military spouse around the world—in fact, we feel like we have lost ourselves in the process. We often hear people say, "When my spouse retires, then it will be my turn."

We don't want you to give up on your dreams. We don't want you to wait twenty years for your turn. This life can be rich and abundant and full of possibilities. It takes an open attitude and a creative approach—along with good friends and a lot of laughter!

The reality is that we do have extreme challenges as military spouses. This is not an easy life! Our path can't be as straightforward as other people's paths might be. That's just the way it is. We have to accept that reality and move forward.

We want to show you what is possible and share the stories of other military spouses who have managed to follow their own dreams as they move around: spouses who have rich, full lives now, not waiting for some future time.

We are all unique individuals. We may all have the military in common, but that's where our sameness stops. There are a lot of ways to live this military life. We each have different talents, interests, priorities, and lifestyle preferences. Some dive fully into military life on post/base while others live their lives more connected to the civilian community. Some of us have wardrobes full of red, white, and blue with "Hooah!" or "Oo-rah!" pins that proclaim our military spouse status and patriotism; others feel just as patriotic and proud to be married to the military but express it in quieter ways.

Every one of us have different life situations as well as different energy levels. If you are married to the military and have no kids, you might take most of what's in this book and run with it. If you have young children at home and are acting as a single parent during a deployment, you might only be able to use bits and pieces of what we cover. We hope you'll at least take the self-care and "how to ask for help" portions to heart for right now and come back to other sections at a later date.

We don't expect every reader to read all parts of the book or even necessarily in sequence. You can start at the beginning or at the end or in the middle. Read what matters most to you!

We write this book and present our workshops with the full understanding that we certainly do not have all the answers. We are constantly learning new things and growing in our own lives and we are always delving into new research. We write this book to share the things we have learned over many years of research and interviewing other spouses—to share the things we wish we had known as new military spouses.

We'd love to see military spouses form groups to work through different reflection and action steps in the book together. We both know the magic and power of groups. We weren't put on this world by ourselves and we don't have to figure out and live this life by ourselves. There's a section in the book on the group process in case you choose to start one.

It's a great idea to get a journal to use as you go through the exercises in later chapters, or to jot down thoughts that trigger as you read.

Have fun with this military life and this process. Approach it all as a grand adventure and that's what you'll experience. Remember, this isn't a dress rehearsal. This is your life. Don't wait to start living it. Take charge now to craft what works for you.

Write to let us know what you do as a result. We love to share stories in our workshops and our writings.

A note about this updated version of the book: So much has happened in our military world since our first edition. We wanted to address some of these changes and to include the most current resources. Some important programs have been created for military spouses and families and we want you to be aware of them. In addition, at the time we wrote our first edition in 2005, we were hopeful that the war in Iraq and Afghanistan and the repeated year-long (and six-month) deployments would come to end. As you well know, this is not so.

Deployments are constant and the anxiety and heartache that comes with the separations never ends (either our loved ones are deployed, gearing up for a deployment, or getting ready to come home from a deployment)—and are huge challenges to overcome. Yet, even in the midst of this, interviews with military spouses continue to verify and document that the things we talk about in this book—friends, support, faith, simple joys, having something for yourself, helping others—are the "only things" that help get you through.

We have expanded our chapters concerning friends, relationships, and support, and faith, hope, and gratitude because these areas have been found to be top answers when asked, "What gets you through the tough times?" These are the cornerstones that carry us through the very challenging times.

Why Purple for Our Cover?

We chose purple for our book cover and workshop logo because purple symbolizes "joint" in the military world, meaning "all services." In the world of color, if you combine Army green, Coast Guard blue, Air Force blue, Marine red and Navy blue, you get purple.

We've seen other meanings to the color purple—many of which relate to the core messages of our workshops and book.

Purple symbolizes:

- a sense of inner calm and feelings of self-worth and inspiration
- knowledge, self-respect, dignity, and wealth

Blue-purple is said to be a spiritual color—the color of truth. It is thought to encourage people to strengthen their values and strive for a higher purpose. The red-purples are considered sensual, exotic, and able to enhance creativity. A blend of dramatic red and calm blue, purple is an "up-for-anything" hue.

We think that is a good description of military spouses—a blend of calm and dramatic and up for anything.

A Short Note about Spouse Stories and Names

We use a mix of first names and full names throughout the book. Where we have permission to use a name, we use it. We know how excited we have been to see our names mentioned in books, and many of the spouses we interviewed said they wanted their full names used too. In some cases, we share stories from the past where we use first names only because we didn't know we would need permission later, and we no longer know how to contact those individuals. For individuals who asked us not to use their names, we've made up a first name and changed other identifying information.

And a Note to the Male Spouses of Female Military Members

The information we share here can be helpful to all military spouses, male and female. However, we know full well that male spouses often face different situations and challenges than we female spouses, and we often face challenges different from yours. Some of what we cover in our book and workshop will apply more specifically to wives. We don't know any way to avoid that. So our stories and examples are mostly female. At the moment, 6 percent of military spouses are male and many of those are prior service so they already know a lot about this military life going into marriage.

We hope there is a male spouse busy writing a book addressing the unique challenges you face, and we'd love to hear from you to be able to share that resource when it's available.

We'd Love to Have You Contact Us!

Please don't think of this book as a one-time resource. Email or call or write us if you:

- have any question that we didn't answer here. If we have the answer, we'll give it to you or at least refer you to a resource. If it might apply to other military spouses, we'll do some added research for you too.
- have a story or example to share that we might use in future books or in our workshops or writings. We will be updating this book as we gather enough new information and stories to share.
- want to start a Dare to Dream Team and want some ideas and help and encouragement along the way.
- would like us to present a workshop in your community (check out our website for current information).

Contact Information:
Website: www.militaryspousehelp.com
Kathie: Kathie@militaryspousehelp.com
Holly: Holly@militaryspousehelp.com
Phone: 503-368-8161 or toll free at 866-JoyJoyJoy (866-569-5695)

Acknowledgments

Okay, these may seem long to some of you. However, our workshops and this book would never have happened without the help of so many people . . . and we want to acknowledge them in print. I would like to thank all the military spouses who have been our biggest supporters and took the time to be interviewed, to share their ideas, give us feedback, and for their ever-so-gentle kick in the pants to stop talking about the book and write it. My admiration and respect for all continues to grow.

I know I would have never survived this crazy lifestyle without my "sisters" to hold my hand during the scary times, to provide a shoulder to lean on, to take care of my children when I needed to help someone else, and for giving me a good belly laugh to get through the day. Sisters such as Deb Alty, Nancy Boatner, Bobby Buxbaum, Christina Clarkson, Robyn Crabtree, Ann Craig, Cheryl Crosswaite, Theresa Donahoe, Anne Donovan, Liz Drago, Erlinda Fiegenbaum, Connie Fullerton, Holly Grange, Dawn Grass, Laura Henry, Ann Marie Irish, Tracy Jameson, Ann Jones, Sandy Kinde, Jen Koprowski, Barbara Loomis, Glenda Luttrell-Williams, Denise Oskvarek, Audrey Osterndorf, Dotty Phipps, Heather Reekie, Vivian Rhoades, Roz Riley, Phoebe Rinkle, Ginger Rivenbark, Tracey Rooney, Trish Rouse, Betty Rutherford, Kathy Schroedel, Sarah Selvidge, Cathy Sterling, Ann Strand, Betsy Talbot, Janette Thomas, Linda Toth, Phyllis Ward, Julie Woods, and Beverly Young.

And a special thanks to my "angels with skin on them." Nancy Wiersma whose humor, intelligence, empathetic spirit, and gourmet cooking helped me survive the first year of my twins' lives when we lived in Germany and my husband was deployed. And for Rhonda Kolesar's willingness to step in and take care of my children as I traveled to provide workshops to military spouses. I couldn't have done this without her help.

I would have never ventured down this road if it weren't for Kathie. She has been able to live the life she preaches and has a remarkable ability to persuade others to live their lives to their fullest potential. I couldn't be more blessed to have her as my friend. I also want to thank Greg Hightower for his ability to make me laugh every time we talk, especially during some of the most difficult times in my life.

My biggest cheerleaders have come from within my own family. My mother's wisdom, encouragement, and perpetual empathetic ear gave me the strength to believe in myself and forge forward in life. My father's pride and love for me is never ending, something I wish every woman could feel. And a big thank you to my in-laws, who were always willing to help out in any way so I could travel and speak to other military spouses.

—HOLLY

This isn't the first book I've talked about writing over the past seventeen years. I thank all those who spent time filling out questionnaires and interviewing with me in the past. Even if those earlier books didn't come to fruition, you were an important part of the process! Thanks to the spouses in our workshops for giving us feedback on what works and what doesn't and for encouraging us to keep doing this work. Thanks to the many spouses who took the time to fill out our lengthy questionnaire and to have individual interviews. Your stories inspire us all.

I couldn't have done any of my speaking and writing business, much less this book, without the support and encouragement and occasional kick in the pants of my many support groups. To the members of my first Tacoma group, the Oregon coast group, the Heidelberg group, BIG group in Corvallis, and my old and new Tacoma groups, you know who you are. Many of your stories are included within these pages. To my many "email/phone buddies" who provide ongoing cheerleading, problem-solving, and support—people like Linda Beougher and the Oregon coast "sisters." Thanks to military spouse friends such as Tanna Schmidli and Cathy Sterling who came to our workshops many times over and became some of our best advocates! We couldn't have written this book or our *Air Force/Army/Marine Corps/Navy Times* column and other articles without the editing help of my Tacoma writers' group. Thanks to Linda Avery, Karen Irwin, Jen See (and to Julianne Johnson for help with my earlier *Army Times* column, and Theresa Donahoe for editing help with this book).

Thanks to my parents for setting the example of connecting to the greater world. They and my sister Nancy gave me good lessons in the rewards of risk-taking.

Thanks to all my speaker friends in the National Speakers Association who have taught me so much about this business. And especially to Joyce Cooper whose encouragement kept me from quitting speaking after my dismal evaluations at my first big women's conference in Seattle 1991. And to Cheryl Vollmer who gave me my first opportunity to present workshops for military spouses—very early on. If you two hadn't believed in me so much I might not have believed in myself.

Thanks to Jan Weir at janweir.net for her wonderful designs for our flyers, website, and the first edition of this book—and for being such fun to work with.

And thanks to Holly. She's the one who first said, "Let's create a workshop to share this great information with other military spouses." We quite frankly figured it didn't matter if we ever gave one workshop, since we had so much fun and learned so much from creating it. I can highly recommend partnering on big projects with a good friend. And talk about dedication—Holly always has the hardest job arranging all the logistics to be able to be on the road and fitting in time late at night to work on the book and the column after the twins have gone to bed. She's taught me how to play. And thanks to Jack Scherer who supported Holly in doing these workshops for spouses even when things got a bit crazy with our travel.

Thanks to Dixie Schneider who filled in when Holly was too sick to do some of the early workshops—Dixie also taught me about loosening up and being more playful.

Thanks to Mary Craig, Kim Gates, and Ginny Greatsinger for ideas that improved our workshop and for the opportunity to meet so many amazing Marine Corps spouses.

And, finally, thanks to Dawn Manchester, an Army spouse who attended one of our workshops in Germany in May 2004. Dawn suggested the first part of the book title: Help! I'm a Military Spouse. We both had an immediate gut reaction of, "That's it!" when we read her suggestion.

—Kathie

Prologue

Why Should I Believe You Two?

"Welcome to the fun and adventure of life as a military spouse." We can just hear you sarcastically saying, "Ha! Yeah . . . right!" as you roll your eyes. That's certainly how we might have reacted to a cheery statement like that early in our married lives. There ought to be a disclaimer when you marry someone in the military—spelling out the hardships you will face along the way. Of course, maybe it's better that we don't know ahead of time.

As we heard one Marine spouse say, "Let's face it, nobody in his or her right mind would sign up for this kind of life." Or, as Elsie Hammond, co-founder of *Military Spouse* magazine says, "I didn't plan on being married to the Navy, but you can't plan love." We marry a person with whom we've fallen in love without much of an idea of what we are taking on.

Oh sure, many women know what this life entails, those who grew up with it perhaps or who were in the military themselves. However, even those who grew up in this life quickly realize there is a big difference between being a military child and being a military spouse, just as there is a big difference in being in the military and being married to the military! Most of us don't really have a clue. Us included.

Kathie's Story

I had some experience with military life before I married into it, so you'd think I'd have known exactly what I was getting into and how to make it work. Wrong.

I grew up as a civil service brat in Berlin and Rhein Main, Germany, and then with my dad working at Fort Belvoir, Virginia. I entered the Army myself right out of college as a Second Lieutenant. After three years on active duty, when my then-fiancé Greg and I were planning on marrying, we were told we'd be stationed in two different places. We decided we didn't want to start our marriage that way, so I left the service and became a "dependent" overnight. I'll never forget the first time I went to sign a check at Fort Rucker, Alabama, as a newlywed. The clerk asked me for "your last four." I gave her the last four of my Social Security Number as I'd been doing for three years. "Well, that doesn't match what is on this check," she said. "Well, that's my husband's last four—you asked for mine." "Well," she said with a roll of her eyes and an exasperated voice, "Of course I meant his last four." Suddenly, I'd lost my identity. I wasn't me anymore; I was a dependent. I obviously didn't count.

I struggled terribly with that dependent status. I wanted respect and acknowledgement of me as an individual, not as a military wife. I wanted to be accepted as a person in my own right, not based on whom I was married to. I found it challenging to find decent jobs with each move. I resented this life more and more. I didn't feel like I fit in as a "good military spouse," often feeling like a black sheep and outsider.

Because I worked full-time and traveled quite a bit on business trips, I couldn't be involved in Greg's units as much as other spouses were. (And yes, in many cases, I simply chose not to be. I admit to having a bit of an "I'm better than this" attitude that isolated me.) Yes, I felt guilty about that and figured people were badmouthing me for not doing more. I didn't have kids, so I didn't feel a part of most spouse conversations at unit functions. In those days, especially, the gatherings tended to split into men/women groups. I found myself drawn to talk with the men, sharing my own "war stories" about my military life—which of course didn't endear or connect me to the wives. Because I wasn't involved, I didn't have friends when I went to those functions, something that made me feel even more alienated. To be quite honest, I dreaded going to unit functions.

During that time, I blamed my unhappiness with my life on the military. I spent a lot of time complaining. Of course, the military is a bit hard to complain to, so guess whom I complained to? Actually, I complained to anyone who would listen to me, but my husband got the brunt.

See if this sounds familiar to you. I'd say things like, "If the military didn't move us so much . . . I'd be able to get that job I want." "If the military didn't move us so much, we could have a garden, but what's the use?" "If the military didn't move us so much, I could do what she's doing over there." I compared my life and myself with other people and came up short in my estimation. Greg used to say to me, "The grass is always greener elsewhere for you, isn't it?" And it was. I wasted a lot of years wallowing in my negative attitudes about this life rather than taking creative action to make changes.

I finally got it that the military wasn't going to change for me, or at least not as fast as I might want. I had to change. I needed to figure out how to make this life work for me—within the challenges of military life. I also realized that the blame didn't really fit totally on the military. I had to take some of the blame for lack of clarity on what I wanted and for my own lack of action. I had to take responsibility.

So I did a lot of research. I read self-help books, listened to tapes, and took a number of personal growth courses. I learned a lot of things I could do to make changes to my life and I started making those changes.

I can tell you now that I love my life and I've been able to say that for a long time. The circumstances didn't change. I changed my attitude and my approach. It works.

Holly's Story

I met my husband, Jack, on a blind date when he was attending a military course in Washington, DC. I was working at Johns Hopkins Hospital in Baltimore, Maryland, and taking graduate courses at Johns Hopkins University. I considered myself intelligent and well educated, but I was totally ignorant about military life.

I fell head over heels in love with Jack. He was the smartest man I had ever met; his morals and ethics were impeccable. Fortunately, he fell head over heels for me too and asked me to marry him on our fourth date. Nine short months later we were married.

I need to preface my story by saying when I was dating Jack, he was attending a military school and I only saw him on weekends. I had never seen his military uniform. I'd had zero experience with anything military. I was clueless. I didn't know that when you marry someone in the military it means you are marrying into a new lifestyle. The military is not a job that someone goes to for forty to seventy hours a week. It is an entirely new lifestyle—a lifestyle I knew nothing about.

Now let me finish my story, I want you to visualize Jack and me back from our honeymoon, living in a tiny duplex in Manhattan, Kansas, and it is my first morning as a military spouse far away from my former East Coast life. It was 4 a.m. and the alarm went off. Certainly it was set for the wrong time, I thought. No, my husband jumped out of bed.

"What are you doing?" I asked. "Getting ready for work," he said matter-of-factly.

"At 4 a.m.?" I gasped in disbelief. He proceeded to put on his camouflage uniform (BDUs, cammies).

"Why are you going to wear that Jungle Man outfit?" I asked curiously.

"This is what I wear everyday to work," he said seriously.

"You have got to be kidding! You wear a jungle man outfit to the office? No way!"

I started to laugh as he slipped on his combat boots and proceeded with the long process of tucking his pant legs into the boots and lacing the boots all the way up and then so carefully tucking the ends of the laces into the boot. Who in the world wakes up at 4 a.m., unless you are a baker or early show TV personality? And certainly no one would put on a Jungle Man outfit, carry a briefcase, and head to the office. Not only did he leave at the crack of dawn that morning as he did every morning for years to come, he also did not come home for dinner, and sometimes not at all because he was working on a project or was off training or deployed for months on end. If you are married to someone in the military I know you can relate.

I've always heard people are unhappy when their expectations do not meet reality. I admit I had expectations of what married life would be like. This reality was not even close to my expectations. Over the next few years I grew unhappy with my life. Even though I adored my husband, I was unhappy that I rarely saw him. I was unhappy about the demands that were placed upon me because of my husband's position in his unit. I was unhappy that the military could tell my husband to go somewhere without me for a year and he had to go— sometimes to dangerous locations. I was unhappy that we had to move so often with no input or choice of where we would go next. I was unhappy that I had to leave my church, my friends, my garden, my home, and my job—the job that took me so long to find each time we moved. I knew I was responsible for my own happiness and I could not expect my husband to be the source of my happiness. But I didn't know how to break this cycle of negativity, always blaming my un- happiness on everything and everybody else.

I was left with this thought. If people are unhappy when their expectations do not meet reality then they have to either change their expectations or change reality.

At times I thought it would be easier to change reality than change my expectations. I struggled with how I could change my expectations without feeling angry or bitter. That's when I met Kathie.

Kathie put it to me bluntly. She said, "Think about it. As a military spouse, you've got three choices about how you want to live your life from this point forward. The choice is yours."

- *Divorce—I could divorce my husband—yes, that is a choice but it wasn't a choice I was willing to make. I adore Jack. He is someone I want to grow old with and I believe in the vows I made on our wedding day. I felt confident divorcing my husband was not a choice that would lead to my happiness in life. (Mind you there are bad marriages in the military just like in civilian life. They should end in divorce, because of the bad relationship, not because of the military.)*
- *Get out of the military—I could convince Jack to get out of the military—but Jack adamantly believed it was his duty to serve his country and felt it was an honor to be a soldier. He had a vision and a plan for his life even before I met him. How could I ask someone I loved to give up something that he believed so deeply in his heart? Not all of us have the calling to serve our country, but thank God there are those who do. I could not imagine asking Jack to give up something he believed so deeply in.*
- *Change my attitude and approach—my third choice was to figure out how to make this life work so I could work toward my dreams. I wanted to see progress toward my dreams as well as my husband's dreams. We were a couple and we needed a joint plan. I had to figure out how to craft a life for me within this military lifestyle.*

Kathie shared what she had discovered to make this challenging lifestyle work. I began to make conscious choices and changes in my life, accepting responsibility for my choices—and lo and behold my life started to change from just an okay life to a life full of joy and richness. I knew we had to share this with others. That's how the workshop and this book got started, at Fort Leavenworth, Kansas, in 1991, during long walks, over coffee, and talking late into the evenings.

Based on the research Kathie had done for herself, and much additional research, we started giving workshops called Joyful Living in 1994. Since then, we've continued our research, and have evolved the workshops even further. We now call them Follow Your Dreams While You Follow the Military™ and we've been presenting workshops to military spouse groups as much as we've been able to for free for three years all over Europe, and later as a business enterprise.

How many workshops we could give has been limited based on our own moves, dealing with deployments, and dealing with family and life challenges. We can't do as many as we get asked to do. So we thought we'd put this information into a book that could reach more spouses.

We want to save other spouses from wasting ten years like we each did, or even one year of this military life. Sure it's hard. Sure there are things that don't seem fair. But there are ways to make it work—and there are some pretty wonderful things about this lifestyle when we open our eyes to them.

Chapter 1

What If I Don't Fit This Life?

The Myth of the Perfect Military Spouse
Versus Authenticity and Uniqueness

Ask any spouse who's been married to the military what preconceived notions they had about the typical military spouse or possibly the "good military spouse," and you'll often hear the myth.

The mythical creature described is a wife who has two children and doesn't work outside the home; or if she does, she cheerfully puts her spouse's career first. She keeps a perfect house with seasonal decorations on the door, moves and settles into new quarters with curtains up in three weeks flat, easily keeps things running at home during deployments, and makes all food from scratch for unit gatherings.

The myth is usually a wife, although we have many men married to women in the military now, and they come in with no set role model of the "perfect military husband." The "norm" for so long was a male military member with a female spouse that that's where these stereotypes developed. And how many of those mythical creatures do you know? In our many years of being married to the military we can't say that we've even met one, but the myth persists.

One thing that perpetuates this myth is the number of spouses, ourselves included, who spend many years trying to fit themselves into some aspect of this myth. We've both spent time trying to dress "right," fix our houses "right," entertain "right," say the "right" things. We were trying so hard to live up to everything we kept hearing in this military world. We often felt like we were black sheep who just didn't fit into this world. We beat ourselves up by comparing our less-than-stellar lives to this mythical ideal. It's certainly not a healthy way to go about your life.

We loved hearing what Cecilia Abrams, wife of Gen. John Abrams, had to say about her own experience. "I remember watching the majors' wives and colonels' wives. I thought to myself, Look at all they do. They run things. They volunteer. They look perfect. They entertain beautifully," she said. "I told my husband we were in trouble; he would not make major because I like to wear sweats and I like to wear them to the commissary."

Another Army spouse, Lynn Edwards, shares the story of the first coffee she held at her house for the unit wives. "I had this image in my head that I had to have china and crystal and a fancy coffee service," says Lynn. "If it had been up to me, I'd have had pizza and soda, but I bought into the myth." Since she worked in the hospitality industry, she was able to borrow all the fancy stuff she wanted. "It was the most uncomfortable evening I've ever had," she continues. "The other wives would have been much happier with pizza and sodas too. I never made that mistake again. I decided to just be myself from then on."

The strength of the military community comes from the wide variety and diversity of its members. It's important to pay attention to your interests and passions whatever they are—and find ways to fit them into this life. It's important to live from the place of your own

> *It's important to live from your own authenticity and uniqueness rather than trying to fit yourself into a mold that isn't you.*

authenticity and uniqueness rather than trying to fit yourself into some mold that isn't you. By figuring out what you need and carving out pieces of what you need—what feeds your soul—you'll change your daily experience of life.

Let's celebrate the fact that we have the great opportunity to interact with such a diverse group of people. As Army spouse Theresa Donahoe says, "One thing I've learned in this lifestyle is to expand my definition of 'friend' in the military spouse arena. I had to learn that just because my initial impression of someone might be that they were 'not my type,' I often found that my 'type' was changing and that I enjoyed a much larger variety of friends than I ever had growing up. People I may never have given myself a chance to know in my old life turned out to become some of my closest and dearest friends." Those diverse friends help you to stretch and grow as you move through this life. We've found that there is a strong bond among military spouses—or at least there can be if you are open to it. We have all entered a life that is different and often difficult for all of us. Connecting with others who are going through the same thing is a big part of that experience.

We aren't saying, "Ignore all conventions!" Don't confuse authenticity with a license to blatantly disregard or disrespect common courtesies. You will encounter many formal occasions during your military life. Remember we have already mentioned that military life is a lifestyle, not a job. We encourage you to find out about the military lifestyle by understanding military traditions. Ask questions and talk with your spouse and others. The formal social occasions that you will be invited to are tied to long military traditions, traditions that feed into the pride and esprit de corps of the military. By learning more about the traditions in this lifestyle you will become more comfortable at formal functions and enjoy being part of tradition. In this chapter we are advocating that you be your authentic self. But the bottom line is don't be stupid. A Change of Command ceremony for your spouse's unit is not the time to show off your new belly-button ring by wearing short shorts and a halter-top. You can show your own authenticity and still be appropriate to the occasion.

What about That Mythical Creature Who Shows Up during Deployments?

Back-to-back deployments have raised the mythical creature again. Here's what we hear—and often what we read about in news articles and see in television interviews. "Military spouses are strong, self-reliant, courageous, independent"— the descriptive list goes on. We are the first to stand up and say military spouses are amazing human beings who manage to handle more than most people will ever be asked to do. However, the key words are: human beings. Human beings get lonely, depressed, scared, lazy, and apathetic during difficult times in their lives, especially during deployments. That is reality and that is okay.

One of the biggest responses on military.com's forums/chat rooms recently was to a topic titled "confessions." The moderator started with her own and added, "We won't judge you."

"I confess that in my husband's absence I've been depressed and lazy. I confess that I don't do the very things that he didn't do and I nagged him for. Like, I don't put my dirty clothes in the hamper all the time. I don't make the bed. I confess I don't shower every day. I don't shave, either—who's going to see my legs?"

She struck a chord. More than three thousand responses poured in.

- "I confess that I've eaten an entire bag of popcorn for dinner on many occasions."
- "I confess that I watch way too much TV and haven't set out to accomplish any of my goals for this deployment (i.e., lose weight, learn to sew, read more.)"
- "I confess that I have been lazy and if it weren't for me having to get up and go to work I would probably never get out of bed."

- "I confess that I cry every night when I am alone in bed."
- "I confess that my son is getting himself ready for school in the mornings and I get up in time to make his lunch and drive him to school in my pajamas and slippers."

It really helps to know you aren't the only one who slips into negative behavior during a deployment. It's not uncommon.

We've both been there. Holly remembers days when she really didn't manage to do more than brush her teeth. Kathie can remember making little agreements with herself, such as, "Today I'll finally leave the house and go to the store," but then she'd break that agreement, hiding out in the house and staying up way too late night after night watching videos or reading. Why shower when you can live in sweats with your hair pulled back and a baseball cap on your head? Why clean the house if you don't plan to have anyone visit?

We don't agree with people who criticize others for these actions and say, "just snap out of it," or who put on a "better than thou" attitude because they are handling the deployment so much better. Deployments are difficult—period! With all the repeated deployments, it can be even more challenging to break out of the cycle of negativity and despair.

What happens, however, is that the longer you let the negative actions (or really, inactions) go on, the harder it is to break the inertia and get yourself showered, dressed, and out of the house. But it's essential to your energy and your sanity. It's important to be aware of that.

The only one who can make changes in your life is you. As one spouse added to the confessions, "I confess I have never felt so negative before. I confess I need to kick myself in the butt and get a move on!" She's right.

That's where friends come in (refer to chapter 3) and where interests of your own are essential.

Here's the good news: if you were meant to do things all by yourself, you would have been put here all by yourself. The fact is, as a human being and military spouse, you are not here on this earth all by yourself. You do not have to do things by yourself. There are people here to help you—and many who are in your shoes need friendship and support as well. It does take some effort on your part to take the step out.

Sometimes we do need someone to kick us into action every now and then—to remind us to get out there and start living again—even in the midst of a deployment. The things we share in this book are exactly the things you can do to start making changes in your life and start living again. If you find yourself stuck in despair, we hope this book will be what you need to help you pull up your bootstraps and get out there and start living your life. And that's exactly what the research on happiness—and interviews with hundreds of spouses—tell us: engaging in life is key to your happiness in life. You can take action toward that. Here's how.

Chapter 2

The Keys to Happiness and What That Means to You

What the Research on Happiness Tells Us about Your Life with the Military

Our workshops and this book are centrally based on the research about what makes a person happy in life. Findings of the American Psychological Association's "Positive Psychology" movement along with results of many other studies point out keys to human happiness and a better quality of life. Happiness is the fulfillment of cherished goals in valued areas of life.

We focus on how you can apply that research to your life with the military. We aren't just sharing this information because it happened to work for us. It has worked for us and other military spouses *and* it's based on research. That means it can work for you too.

When we shared this information in our workshops, people would say, "Isn't it simply genetic to a great degree? Aren't some people just plain happier, more easy-going, than others?"

Simply look around at your friends and family and you'll probably agree with this concept. And it's true. We see it with the two of us. Holly is an optimistic, cheerful, playful, "glass is half full" kind of person and always has been. Kathie comes from a pessimistic family tending toward a negative, anxious, "glass is half empty" approach to life. Research explains why.

Studies from the University of Minnesota conclude that about 50 percent of one's satisfaction with life comes from genetic programming. Genes influence such traits as having an easy-going personality, ability to deal with stress, and feeling low levels of anxiety and depression (Lykken 1996). David Lykken found that circumstantial factors like income, marital status, religion, and education contribute only about 8 percent to one's overall well being. The remaining 42 percent can be influenced by your own thoughts and actions. Your choice of focus. Your attitude. (So what our book and workshop go after is that 42 percent—the area you can make conscious choices to change.)

Key findings from the happiness research point out how greatly the following five areas impact your happiness—your overall quality of life. We'll discuss each in brief here and then in later chapters we'll expand on each one—to show how you can make changes in each area to increase your own quality of life.

- Support—Relationships,
- Faith, Hope, and Gratitude,
- Simple Joys,
- Action Toward What You Want,
- Service.

First Key to Happiness: Seek Out Friends and Support

Ask any military spouse who has been through a deployment or other challenge of military life, "What helped you get through that time?" and you will probably hear the answer, "my friends." Spouses who have the hardest time with military life are those isolated by circumstances or who choose to isolate themselves.

Relationships are key to our happiness in life, during deployments and otherwise. A study conducted at University of Illinois (Diener and Seligman 2002) found the most common characteristic shared by those who have the highest levels of happiness and the fewest signs of depression are those who have strong ties to friends and family and a commitment to spending time with them. All the research we found concluded the happiest people are those who have strong relationships and strong support structures. That can be your spouse, your family, your friends, a church group, or other kinds of groups. Because of the importance of this, we'll look at how to make friends and to stay connected with friends as you move with the military, along with ways to strengthen your relationship with your spouse.

Second Key to Happiness: Cultivate Faith

Faith is another essential key to overall happiness in life. The majority of the happiness research indicates that a belief in something greater than yourself provides the sense of hope that is key to overcoming challenges in life. And that sense of hope is crucial to our sense of well-being.

Sermons and sacred texts of various religions and ethnic groups have long promised those who are faithful rewards of inner peace, comfort, joy, and a sense of well-being. Recently more and more scientific research has been published on the relationship between faith and mental health. The findings from these studies indicate people of faith are less depressed, less anxious, and less suicidal than those who do not have a belief of a Greater Power (something greater than yourself). The studies continue to indicate those of faith are better able to cope with such crises as illness, divorce, and bereavement.

Holly likes to compare our lives at times to a wild storm on the ocean, with waves crashing against the shores and ships tossing back and forth. Yet even in the midst of the storm, if you go down to the depths of the ocean you'll find centers of calm and stillness. The waves and what's on top of the water represent our outer lives—constantly busy and sometimes absolutely crazy. Yet, like the depths of the ocean, we too have a stillness and quiet within us that we can get to even in the midst of a storm. Individuals who have a strong faith and regular spiritual practice, who allow themselves to get quiet and go within on a regular basis, find they touch a center of calm that helps carry them through the stormy times. We've talked to many military spouses who say that their faith actually deepened during deployments. We'll look at ways that military spouses find to access that stillness. We'll also consider the importance of gratitude in our daily lives well as during times of challenge. Taking the time to switch our focus to what we are grateful for can make a difference in how we experience and approach our situations in life.

Faith provides a sense of hope that is key to overcoming challenges in life.

Third Key to Happiness: Discover Simple Joys

The research shows that our experience of happiness in life to a great degree is made up of simple daily joys. It's a matter of learning to "be in the moment" enough to enjoy simple pleasures as they occur. Many of us have a lot of joy in our lives, but often are racing right by what is good as we move right on to the next task, to the next item on our daily "to-do" list. We can greatly improve our daily quality of life—and our energy—by taking time to participate in and appreciate very simple joys. We'll look at how you can do that in your life along with some other ways to increase your daily energy and decrease your stress.

Fourth Key to Happiness: Know What You Want and Take Action to Achieve It

The happiest people know what they want their lives to be like and they are working to achieve that vision in some manner. What's really interesting about this aspect of happiness is that it is not achieving your big dream that brings happiness. What brings you joy is that you have identified what you want in line with your values and you are taking action to get it. You are taking control of and responsibility for your own destiny instead of letting things happen to you. You are not stuck waiting for some future event or timing, not waiting for "someday," not waiting for your spouse's retirement. You have a real sense of self and are engaged in life. That's what brings the joy. It's the process itself, enjoying the journey.

Understanding this concept and acting on it was the big turning point for us when we started our searches for a different life within this military lifestyle. Until that point, we had been letting life happen, not making conscious choices and not taking responsibility to change things that weren't working. We both used the military and those constant moves as the excuse for not pursuing what we really wanted in life.

What's interesting is that people accepted that excuse. So did we. But when we really looked at it more objectively, we each realized there were many military spouses doing what we said we wanted to do—and many of those spouses had much bigger challenges than we did.

That's when we started making conscious choices, setting goals and taking action, taking responsibility, finding ways around all these obstacles we'd been allowing to stop us. We finally opened ourselves up to possibility thinking and abundance thinking rather than wallowing in impossibility and lack.

The experiences of other military spouses support this positive approach to this military lifestyle. Here's what other military spouses have to say. "It's not an easy life, but it can be very rewarding if you take control of each assignment and make the most of it," says Christina Clarkson, an Army spouse whose twins were three and her older child was five when her husband deployed as a unit First Sergeant. "It's a shame to see spouses who are so frustrated with their lives but don't step out to make things better."

Angie was brand new to active Army life and had just arrived in Baumholder, Germany, with her husband, three children, and a brand new baby. Three days later they found out her husband was deploying. She was miserable the whole time he was gone, hanging out with other unhappy wives, complaining about life, gossiping, and generally stuck in negativity.

"I realize now the reason I was so unhappy there was because I didn't have any dream or purpose of my own," Angie says. "Now I do." At the time we talked with Angie, she was graduating from the Gene Juarez nail school, going on for advanced training and a guaranteed job at their Tacoma salon. "I have bigger dreams of owning my own day spa," she adds. "I've got my husband thinking of the future too, so we are saving to buy property some day."

Amy J. Fetzer is a Marine spouse, mother of three children, and author of more than thirty novels and novellas. She's been involved with the military community, moved many times, lived overseas, and still managed to carve out something for herself. "The best way to have a happy life with the military is to have something that you do for yourself," says Amy. "Establishing yourself, your work as an individual in an Armed Service where individuality isn't the norm means not just being a wife or mother. I was each of those things, still am, but I was always a writer too. It gave me the separation as a person that I needed to be happy with who I was." When you have something for yourself, she adds, those times alone won't seem so lonely.

> *The best way to have a happy life with the military is to have something that you do for yourself."*
> —*Amy J. Fetzer, Marine spouse*

Silke Hagee, wife of Gen. Michael Hagee, 33rd Commandant of the U.S. Marine Corps and proud Marine spouse for more than thirty-five years agrees. She loves music and plays the cello. She says her music has been a lifesaver for her. The cello has given her something continuous throughout all the deployments and relocations. Playing the cello allowed her to hook up with an orchestra, a trio, or a quartet at every duty station, even in 29 Palms in 1973–74 when 29 Palms was literally twenty-nine palms!

Her music gives her great joy because it is all hers. She stressed how important it is to have something in your life that makes you your own person. "Most of the time we are someone to someone else, the wife, the mother, the daughter. Find an interest that is all yours."

The key here is to carve out pieces of your dream as you move with the military—and to fight for those pieces. That way you'll be ready to grow them even further when you do stop moving. Do something that feeds your soul, starting now!

There is another important reason to have something you do for yourself. Many spouses told us that it was that interest—whether it was a job they loved or a hobby like scrap booking or quilting or a community project they were intensely involved in—that helped them through deployment. As one woman said, "It saved my sanity. For at least a few hours each day, I could manage to forget about Iraq. It kept the constant anxiety at bay."

In chapter 7 we'll show you ways to help you figure out what you want—and then start taking action—right now toward it.

Fifth Key to Happiness: Work from Your Strengths to Serve a Greater Good

The research suggests and our experience and interviews with many military spouses confirm that the greatest "high" in life comes from using your strengths to serve a greater good. There really is such a thing as a "helper's high" similar to the "runner's high" where the release of endorphins, the feel-good brain chemicals, increase our experience of happiness. The most lasting experience of happiness occurs from using our strengths in service to others. That can be one-on-one with a child, with coworkers in the workplace, in a volunteer situation, or with a stranger on the street.

Holly's experience and training in the special education field have taught her the importance of finding the gifts or strengths in each individual and then figuring out a way to build on those strengths. We all have been given gifts/strengths. Everyone—guaranteed! It's these gifts/strengths that help to define your role in life.

Note to Parents: The greatest gift we can give our children is to help them identify their strengths and to help them nurture and build on those strengths. Teach them to listen within for guidance and encourage them to use those strengths to help others in this world. It's the greatest gift we can give ourselves as well—identifying and building on our strengths for the greater good. Doing this gives any individual a sense of purpose in life.

Like so many military spouses, Army spouse Cathy Sterling tells us the "helper's high" is what keeps her going. Cathy has been volunteering countless hours, year after year in the different military communities where she has lived. We sit back in awe at her willingness to continuously and cheerfully help other military spouses. Here's the deal. Cathy is using her strengths to help others and the end result is this "helper's high." Cathy says, "I know I have a choice of where I use my strengths and I want to be involved in my community, knowing that I might be helping others through my actions. The bottom line is I feel a sisterhood with other spouses and they are the ones that keep me going."

It took Cathy awhile to realize that finding your purpose or your calling could be as simple as recognizing that you may already be doing what you are supposed to be doing. Often our purpose and happiness in life are right in front of us if we just stop and take notice.

In review, five key factors in your overall happiness in life are:
- Support—Relationships,
- Faith, Hope, and Gratitude,
- Simple Joys,
- Action Toward What You Want,
- Service.

We'll look at these factors in greater detail, at how you can apply this knowledge to your own life as you move and grow with the military.

Resources

14,000 Things to Be Happy About, by Barbara Ann Kipfer (1990).

Authentic Happiness: Using the New Positive Psychology to Realize Your Potential for Lasting Fulfillment, by Martin Seligman, Ph.D. (2002).

Frugal Luxuries: Simple Pleasures to Enhance Your Life and Comfort Your Soul, by Tracey McBride (1997).

Happiness: The Nature and Nurture of Joy and Contentment, by David T. Lykken, (2000).

Happiness: What Studies on Twins Show Us about Nature, Nurture, and the Happiness Set Point, **(the 2006 info was from an article about his research, so maybe we should use the 2000 date in the sentence reference instead).** by David T. Lykken, (1999).

How Full Is Your Bucket? Positive Strategies for Work and Life, by Tom Rath and Donald O. Clifton, Ph.D. (2004).

Managing to Have Fun, by Matt Weinstein (1996).

Quality of Life Therapy: Applying a Life Satisfaction Approach to Positive Psychology and Cognitive Therapy, by Michael B. Frisch (2006): Note, this is an academic volume. His companion book for the general public is *Finding Happiness with Quality of Life Therapy: A Positive Psychology Approach* (2006).

Simple Abundance: A Daybook of Comfort and Joy, by Sarah Ban Breathnach (1995).

The Antisocial Personalities, by David T. Lykken (2006).

The Woman's Comfort Book, The Couple's Comfort Book, Comfort Secrets for Busy Women, and other books, by Jennifer Louden (1992, 1994, 2004).

Very Happy People, by Edward Diener and Martin Seligman, Ph.D. (Psychological Science, vol. 13, 2002).

What Happy People Know: How the New Science of Happiness Can Change Your Life for the Better, by Dan Baker, Ph.D., and Cameron Stauth (2003).

Wishcraft: How to Get What You REALLY Want, and other books, by Barbara Sher (1979).

You Don't Have to Go Home from Work Exhausted, by Anne McGee-Cooper, Ph.D., and colleagues (1992).

Chapter 3

Seek Out Friends and Support

How to Make Friends and Stay
Connected as You Move

During the question and answer period at a library "Meet the Author" event, Army spouse Shequita Gatlin stood up and asked Kathie, "How do you make friends when you are new other than knocking on doors and looking weird?"

Her question prompted us to add this chapter to our book. Since the research shows that "positive social relationships"—friendships—are a key ingredient to human happiness, we need to know how to make friends. And as military spouses, we can't just do that once. In our mobile lifestyle, even more than for most people, we have to do what our old Girl Scout song taught us, "to make new friends and keep the old." The fact is that military spouses who are isolated by circumstances or who choose to isolate themselves will have the most difficult time with this lifestyle. And the reality is that some of those who are isolated are often isolated because they are introverts and don't know how to go about making friends. Friends are important for our happiness and they affect our ability to deal with stress.

Friendships during stressful times might be even more important for women. A landmark UCLA study (Taylor et al. 2000) suggests that women respond to stress with a cascade of brain chemicals, an increase in oxytocin. The study showed that the hormone oxytocin buffers the fight or flight stress response we've always heard of and encourages women to tend their children and gather with other women instead. These "tend and befriend" activities counter stress and produce a calming effect. This doesn't occur for men because their higher levels of testosterone counter the effect of oxytocin in their systems. Men tend instead to respond to stress in true "fight or flight" behavior—by becoming aggressive or withdrawing.

So what does that mean to military wives? Hanging out with your girlfriends is not a luxury in times of stress. It's a necessity! It's a scientific fact! So if you've been putting friendships on the back burner while you focus all your time and energy on everyday demands of life, think again.

Our friends are important parts of our lives. As Marla Paul, author of *The Friendship Crisis: Finding, Making, and Keeping Friends When You're Not a Kid Anymore* says: "Friends assuage our guilt, ease our stress, make us laugh, recharge our energy, carry our grief and celebrate our successes."

> *Hanging out with your girlfriends in times of stress is a necessity. It is a scientific fact.*

Here's another thing to consider. Dr. Pamela Peeke, author of *Fight Fat Over 40*, has led groundbreaking work on the link between chronic stress and weight gain. She has found that women under stress often have another response: "Stew and chew." We expect this is applies even more to those spouses who are isolated. If you hold all your stress in, worry about everything, and eat to deal with that stress, you end up still stressed—and heavier, which for most of us just adds more stress! Hanging out with positive friends is a much better option.

Making friends really is a skill you can learn—and as a military spouse, you get a lot of opportunity to practice doing so. Let's look at some ways.

Find Other Newcomers

Most posts/bases have newcomer orientation programs. These are helpful ways to quickly discover what resources and facilities are available in your new community. Overseas they also help you to learn the new customs and logistics of life in a foreign land. And they are an easy place to make new friends since everyone there is also new and most likely looking to connect.

Another place to find newcomers is with newcomers groups off base or post. Check out the Newcomers and Moms Worldwide Directory at www.newcomersclub.com for listings by state and by country.

As Army spouse Martha Klinck says, "Ten years and eight moves later, I have found that the easiest way for me to make friends was with those people arriving at post at the same time. In the U.S., it is especially difficult to break into established 'circles.' Overseas it tends to be much easier to make friends—'We are all in the same boat together.'"

Attend Activities That Interest You and Talk with People

We looked back on how we met our many military and civilian friends and we asked many other spouses to do the same. One common way that people meet new people is by participating in activities that interest them. You'll meet like-minded people. From attending book readings to taking Spanish classes to joining the biking or hiking club, it's a win/win scenario. You get to do something you enjoy and you might meet a new friend. (And even when you don't meet a new friend, you still can engage in something that interests you which ups your happiness in life, so what's to lose?)

As Army spouse Linda Beougher says, "I have found that my best friends appeared when I was doing what I loved to do. That could be taking a class in something that interests me, exercise, a trade group, spending time at my children's school, at the church, whatever. It seemed that I bonded most with people with similar interests/lifestyles more than with people in the unit or neighborhood where I always looked first."

One of Holly's greatest gifts when her twins were young was to be part of a neighborhood playgroup. Gathering together with other moms who were going through the same challenges was affirming. The opportunities for her children to have fun with other children and for her to observe how they played and interacted with other children were benefits in and of themselves. There were others. She could observe how other mothers dealt with parenting issues such as disciplining, which gave her great ideas on how she could approach disciplining her own children. She gathered ideas and resources such as who were the best babysitters in the neighborhood and where to get the best buy on diapers, formula, or hand-me-down clothes. It also became a fabulous support group for her as she listened and shared the ups and downs of parenting with other moms. To top it off, she met one of her dearest friends to this day in her neighborhood playgroup.

If there's not an organized playgroup right now where you are, consider starting one. Inviting another mom and her children over for a play date is the first step. Other places Holly found other moms of young children when she moved to a new area were through an international organization call MOPS (moms of preschoolers)—check out www.mops.org. Now they even have www.militarymops.org.

Don't forget to check out the programs on post/base for young children. All you need to do is strap your child in a stroller and roll on down to your Military Family Service Center and ask what's available for parents and children on base/post. For example, at McChord AFB and Fort Lewis, you'll find The Escape Zone and Raindrops and Rainbows respectively, indoor locations full of activities and toys where moms can gather with their children and connect with each other—even on rainy days.

For many activities you enjoy, you will find groups already in place as you move around. It's an easy entrée into a group of like-minded folks. As one example, if you enjoy knitting, check out www.stitchnbitch.org to find a group of knitters wherever you move. And if you've been thinking about knitting, you should know that they welcome beginners. Working with needles and yarn has been shown to lower stress and blood pressure and lessen pain!

One added thought: You don't even have to attend an event. Just be open to things that interest you. Kathie has met a number of good friends by calling them up after reading an article about them in the post or local newspaper or reading an article they wrote in the paper. She simply asks if they'd be interested in a walk and talk or in meeting over coffee. To date, no one has said no. "You quickly know if there is any kind of connection or not in a first time meeting," she adds. "Some of those meetings were one-time things. Others have evolved into deep, long-term friendships."

Attend activities provided by your spouse's unit. Almost every spouse we talked with for this chapter mentioned at least one good friend they met through their spouse's unit. That is indeed how we met one another—when our spouses were both attending a military school together.

"My first military friend I met through our Battalion Coffee Group," says Army spouse Tara Crooks. "I always tell the story of me moving to Fort Hood, Texas, before Kevin was there (one year early) due to him doing his schooling. I worked for Nine West Group, Inc., in Austin, Texas, and lived in Killeen. I had never been on a post other than Fort Sill as a 'drive-by' and so I was terrified of the commissary and the PX and had no idea what the 'military' was all about. I spent an entire year working my tail off long hours so that I didn't have to go home because frankly I was *lonely*!!! When Kevin finally came to Fort Hood and we joined a unit, the battalion commander's wife was so wonderful! She personally called and introduced herself and invited us to her home. I think if she hadn't done that I never would have gotten involved in coffees and other events in the battery or battalion but thankfully she did. I met my first friend, Erin Nauman, there. Her husband and mine worked together and ironically were very good friends, though we didn't know. We spent our four years in Texas hanging out and exploring with the Naumans.

"Since that time, I have recognized the value of social events in the Army (military)," Tara adds, "and I attend Officers' Spouses Club, Family Readiness Group, battery and battalion functions, balls, etc. You never know what you might find once you're there. It's definitely out of comfort zone but it's helpful."

Connect with Other Military Spouses during Deployments

You might want to take part in military support groups, especially during deployments. You'll connect with others dealing with the same kinds of challenges you are dealing with—and you'll get information about the unit that you might not otherwise get.

· If you are considering moving home during a deployment, you might re-consider. As Marine spouse Tina McIntosh wrote in a recent *Times* newspaper essay, "I thought coming home would be easier and less aggravating. I was wrong." Tina moved home to Ohio when her husband deployed to Iraq. "I had no idea that things would be this different away from a military base or that people were oblivious to world events. I assumed people respected our troops and were as educated as we are. I was wrong. It seems as if they don't even realize there are troops abroad in hostile environments." As she and many other spouses have learned, it can be difficult to be in a civilian environment where everyone is simply going about their lives as "business as usual," as if there were no war going on and no Americans like your spouse living in daily danger.

It really does help to interact with others who are dealing with what you are dealing with. Other friends and family can be sympathetic and supportive, but nobody can really understand what you are going through unless they have done so themselves. Consider these comments from women at a recent retreat for spouses dealing with a year-long Iraq deployment:

- This weekend has taught me that I'm not alone in this situation and that my son is not the only little boy that doesn't like to listen and is not so well behaved. Now I feel like I will be able to make it.
- Being military, as we all know, is nothing like the civilian sector, and I believe that it is great to be able to come together to share, open up, and relate to others in our same "family."
- The best part of the weekend was spending time with other spouses who you know are feeling and going through the same thing as you are. To be able to share feelings and be able to just cry when there was the need. To have people around who understand exactly how I feel and have been feeling for a whole year!

As Navy spouse Erin wrote: "The Norfolk Navy Wives are wonderful! If you need an ear or shoulder at 1 a.m., they are there. If a ride is needed, babysitting, a party, BBQ, or just shopping with a buddy, they are there."

When Army spouses Cathy Sterling, Clara Bergner, Carol Brooks, and Ellen Torrance lived at Fort Stewart, Georgia, they said they couldn't have made it through those days and months of deployments without their "walking talking" buddies. They met in the morning to walk and talk. They claim they would "solve all the world's problems" during those regular walks. They held each other accountable and supported each other. The exercise was an added bonus.

Consider doing what four Marine spouses did during a long deployment. Two of them would take all the kids for an evening and overnight at one house.

The other two women would then have the evening to enjoy a movie and dinner with each other. The next morning these mothers would wake up on their own schedule—no children to feed or get ready. The one night and morning of no responsibilities were absolute luxuries for each of these busy moms. The next week they would reverse roles.

There's another reason that military friends can be so important during a deployment. It's common that your friends who are also dealing with a deployment almost become a surrogate family. You do so many things together—from dinner to watching television to spending time with your kids—that you would otherwise be doing with your spouse. When your spouses return, you both immediately understand that the intensity and time available to spend with one another simply will not be the same. Your civilian friends might not be as quickly understanding of that sudden change.

Being a military spouse allows you an opportunity to become part of a sisterhood that will last a lifetime. This is definitely how Holly talks about her military spouse friends: it's a sisterhood. She never imagined her life would be blessed with so many strong, courageous, self-sacrificing women. This sisterhood welcomed her with open arms from the first day she arrived at Fort Riley, Kansas, as a new bride many years ago. Although the faces in this sisterhood changed constantly as she moved all over the world with her husband and family, the bond these military spouses felt remains rock solid even today.

She would tell others, "If we were meant to be on this earth by ourselves, we would have been put here by ourselves. Here's a news flash. We are not here by ourselves; we are not expected to go through this life by ourselves." This sisterhood believes in helping each other along the way and not worrying about whether or not we are able to repay that person who helped us during a difficult time. Our job would then be to help someone else when we saw an opportunity to do so. As Kathie would say, borrowing from the book of that name, *Pay It Forward*. That's how it works. We help other military spouses and they help others and the cycle of community never stops.

Gather with your positive friends to reduce your stress and increase your happiness. One word of caution. Don't just surround yourself with people only to be around people. Look for positive people. If you are someone like Holly who is very empathetic, she found that negative people would drain her energy. When you are living in this challenging military

> *If we were meant to be on this earth by ourselves, we would have been put here by ourselves.*

lifestyle, you need all the energy you can muster. Sure, we all need the opportunity to vent frustrations, but the last thing we need is to be surrounded by negative, constantly complaining people who can pull us into their negative spirals and cause added stress.

Don't Limit Yourself to Activities on Post or Base

It's great to have a mix of friends, both military and civilian, to enrich your life. Many military spouses have discovered what we have over time: we need our military friends because they truly understand what we are dealing with as we face a deployment or yet another move. They speak our language and can share important resources available through the military. But we also want our civilian friends because they quickly connect us to community resources we might not find otherwise, they take us away from the constant "diet" of military news, and they enrich our lives by exposing us to new worlds outside the "gate." Plus, we think it's important that we all connect more with the civilian community so that there isn't such a divide between our military and civilian worlds.

Be open to connections as you go about your daily routine. Kathie can point out good friends she met sitting next to each other at a workshop, talking on the telephone when Kathie called a local Mac Club for computer help, and going for a chiropractic adjustment.

Army spouse Tara shares this story: "I also have a best friend who lives in the town right outside of post about thirty minutes from me now. When I lived in the same town, I shopped at the local Wal-Mart. We were new here, about two weeks into our tour. We were both standing in line to get pictures. I had my daughter, Wrena (four years old), in the cart and she had her son, Zane, in the cart with her. It was a long line and we stood there forever. I just started up a conversation. Once she walked away I thought, man, I should have gotten her phone number. Lo and behold, two minutes later she came back and she said, 'I really should have gotten your phone number.' Turns out we're both from the Midwest, our kids love each other, our husbands are friends, and we do tons of family things together. It's great to have them here with us at Fort Stewart."

Too Shy to Speak Up?

So . . . what if you are shy? Well, for one thing, you aren't alone. Fifty percent of Americans label themselves as shy. Like many of them have, you can learn to be more comfortable by learning new skills and behaviors (and self-talk). Even those people who aren't shy can learn from this information.

Tap into resources that help you connect. A favorite book of ours is a book by Anne Baber and Lynne Waymon called *Smart Networking* (formerly *Great Connections*) and their follow-up book, *Make Contacts Count*. Both are filled with ideas of how to start conversations, join groups already in conversation, and how to get and keep connections going. The authors share how to remember names, how to leave a conversation when it's time to do so, how to help people remember your name, and how to ask questions that trigger conversations. Kathie credits those books with helping her move past her introverted nature to connect with people with each new move and in each new group situation.

A new book, *The Friendship Crisis: Finding, Making, and Keeping Friends When You're Not a Kid Anymore* by Marla Paul, is also full of great ideas. Paul first wrote an essay about how difficult it was to make new friends with her own move from Dallas to Chicago. When the essay ran in the *Chicago Tribune* and later in *Ladies' Home Journal,* the response was overwhelming. Women across the country wrote in with similar experiences. Using feedback from many of those women along with interviews with top friendship experts, Paul started writing a monthly column on the subject. That column turned into the book. It's a great resource.

For one thing, it's great to see how others have faced the same kind of friend challenges that we all have at some time—from rejection of our overtures to having a clingy too-needy or negative friend to having friends who never take the initiative.

Here are some tips from these books and other resources:

Create Your "Agenda"

This idea from Baber and Waymon is what Kathie, a "recovering introvert," uses to help her step into any new situation where she doesn't know people, and even to help her start meaningful conversations in situations where she may simply not know people very well. Before going for a coffee or to a military ball or to a conference, she takes the time to come up with her agenda. Taking a minute to think about who will be at that event, she comes up with three bits of information that she has to share that might be of interest to people there, and three bits of information she is looking for that those individuals might be able to provide her.

"I don't always need to use my agenda," she says, "since sometimes great conversations just happen. But when we start talking about the weather, this gives me a topic to introduce that just might trigger a more purposeful conversation."

> ### Use the Agenda Idea for a Great Unit Coffee
> —*a way to get everyone talking in a purposeful manner—extroverts and introverts alike.*
>
> *(Here's the actual flyer copy from one of Kathie's unit coffees. Their group used this a couple of times a year to spark resource sharing and conversation. Feel free to tweak it to fit your group and*

location. This would work well in a new neighborhood as well, as a way to get neighbors together to connect and share.)

The Monthly Coffee: Good food, great company (and, yes, let's admit it, getting to check out other people's homes) . . . and most importantly, great resource sharing!

So, join us on___at___. You can come empty-handed, but you have to bring two things in your head (and you might want a pen and paper handy). This will be an opportunity to give and get great resources.

Here's how it works: here's who will be here—military spouses who include working women, stay-at-home moms, childless women, young women, women of a certain age, military, nonmilitary, women who have lived in this area for awhile or in an earlier assignment, women new to the area. You come prepared with one resource (or more if you like) to share and one to ask for.

For example, for me, I'm happy to share:

1. a great and reasonably priced place to buy large and small pots for your indoor and outdoor plants, and, 2. an even nicer place than Ruston Way to enjoy long walks along the water. And resources I'm looking for: 1. best way/place to sell antique furniture, specifically a couch and chair, and, 2. favorite local nurseries.

You get the idea. Here are other possible categories to get you thinking: best free thing to do with kids in the area, best cheap eats restaurant, favorite Washington state ferry route, best home décor store, best military lodging deal in the Northwest or Hawaii. If we find time to share just one resource per person and to get one resource for each person there that evening, just think of all the great resources we'll all discover.

Be Curious

Every person has a story. Learn to ask questions to draw them out—and learn to listen. Ask things like "How did you and your husband meet?" "Is there a story behind your name (for unusual names especially but even more common names often have an interesting story behind them), "What's the best thing that's happened to you in the last week?" "What do you like best about this location?"

Paul's book shares important friendship boosters and friendship busters. The busters include jealousy and habitually canceling dates, for example. The boosters include showing up for happy and sad events, remembering birthdays, artful listening, making peace with imperfection, and helping out in a crisis.

We have always heard that "a friend in need is a friend indeed." It's true. As Army spouse Linda shares, "I have found that my best friends were the ones there for me during difficult times. As much as I thought I could earn a friend from helping them, it was really when I asked for help that I discovered the true meaning of friendship. One of my current best friends is another mom from my child's class a few years ago. Although I didn't know her at the time, I asked if my child could play with hers for a couple of hours while I went to a doctor's appointment. It turned out that I had a major illness and she helped me get through it by taking my children a lot until I could make other arrangements—and our friendship grew. Another friend flew all the way across the U.S. to stay with me and drive me to daily radiation appointments! Thank God for girl-friends and the sacrifices they make."

Ask for a Job

As an introvert, Kathie learned to always "ask for a job" at events and gather-ings. It's much easier for a shy person to initiate conversations with others when they have a purpose: "Please fill out this name tag," "Let me show you where to put your coat," and so on. Volunteering in any community or organization is a sure-fire way to more easily connect.

Find or Create Your Tribe!

Consider forming your own group for support. These groups can take many different forms. Some of you have discovered this joy and support with playgroups, book clubs, or scrap booking groups. There are movie groups and meal-making groups. Check out the book *Girls Night Out,* in which authors Tamara Kreinin and Barbara Camens share stories of women's groups of all shapes, sizes, and ages. Additional information on groups can be found in chap-ter 12 of this book with our Dare to Dream team concept.

The common thread these groups all share is a consistent, planned, and scheduled way to gather together for sharing and laughter. Groups help you to see that you aren't alone and that you aren't the only one who's ever gone through what you are going through. Groups give you support and celebration and a sanity check.

If you are isolated by circumstances, cyber groups can be a lifesaver. Ac-cording to Paul, "Friendships often flourish more quickly over the Internet as some women seem more comfortable revealing themselves on computer screen than in person. It inspires self-revelation in the way of a journal or diary." And you can do this without having to coordinate schedules. There are lots of mili-tary spouse chat rooms. One great place to check is at www.cinchouse.com. Just don't forget the dangers of cyberspace, especially spending too much time chatting and not enough time "living" with your family and local friends, and with taking time for you.

And when your spouse isn't deployed consider the value of groups of couples as friends. We can each point out how much more we enjoyed our assignments when we had that kind of group. We were part of one together in Fort Leavenworth, Kansas, our "Four Seasons Group," a group of military members and their spouses. We shared dinners out and in, wine tastings, day trips around the area, 10K runs, and even a New Year's weekend away where we all joined in the Polar Bear club swim for the New Year's Day! Kathie and Greg have a group in Tacoma now who share dinners and movies out, activities such as bike riding and hiking, and who celebrate milestone events as a group, from baby showers to new jobs.

This can be as simple as finding one common interest and taking turns to take the initiative to share that activity. Army spouse Anne Melia and her husband shared regular "Cheap Eats Nights" with another couple. "One of us would call every three weeks or so and say, 'It's time for cheap eats,'" she says. "It allowed us great conversation time and an opportunity to discover good inexpensive restaurants in the Fort Lewis area."

How Do You Make Time for Your Friends?

Obviously, this is a big challenge for military spouses especially those dealing with a deployment or a move.

One idea is to do your daily activities together. Kathie always suggests a walk whenever someone wants to get together with her. (She used to suggest a run.) "The most consistent I ever was with a running buddy was at Fort Lee, Virginia," she says. "Pat's husband worked with my husband. With three children, one of whom had special needs, the only time she could manage consistently was very early morning before her husband left for work. We would meet and run and talk together. I can't tell you how many times we'd both have trouble dragging ourselves out of bed. We'd say 'I was hoping you'd call to cancel,' but neither of us wanted to let the other down. And we always felt better after the run."

Take a class together, schedule your manicures or pedicures together (Kathie always finds the local beauty school and meets friends there for inexpensive pampering and conversation), or walk your dogs together.

"I strap on my headset for long chats with my friends," says Claire, an Air Force spouse. "I can fold laundry and pick up the house at the same time and still be very present to the conversation."

Trade out things you don't like doing. For example, three of you can help one friend clear out her cupboards or sort her photos into groupings or clean the house together. Then do a dreaded chore for another one the next week. Any chore is easier when done as a team. Good music, conversation, and laughter help you forget that what you are doing is a chore.

The Internet has been a godsend for military spouses. Now, when you first move to a new place, even before you can make new connections, you still have the support of your close friends from the previous assignment. Where you might not be able to afford to talk by phone as often as you might need during those early months, you can email.

"Email is my favorite method of staying in touch, especially with time zone differences," says Linda, "but I still need to hear my friends voices periodically. I have just discovered SKYPES, www.skypes.com, and am thrilled to talk over my computer for free!"

Army spouse Tara Crooks keeps up-to-date with family and friends using on-line blogs. She has a family blog and a personal and professional blog. Other spouses use family websites or family newsletters to keep their friends and family up–to-date with their lives.

And of course the key is to "make time." Value your friendships for what they are and how important they are in your life—for your stress management and more importantly for your happiness. As Marla says, "Treat a friendship like the gift it is."

Make and Keep Friends for Life

One thing many of us have discovered as military spouses is how great it is to have friends worldwide. As we move or travel for business or pleasure, we often have friends to visit—and vice versa. We noticed that with military friends especially, even when many years have passed in between visits, we fall immediately into comfortable deep conversations as if no time had passed. If you've ever been to one of the military resorts like the Hale Koa in Hawaii, you've probably noticed the number of obviously retired couples sitting at dinner and talking and laughing with other older couples. We always picture ourselves doing that in later years, taking advantage of military hops and military resorts to travel with our longtime military friends—as long as we keep the connections strong.

Listen to what Air Force spouse Dixie Schneider says years after her husband retired from the Air Force. "We have friends that we made in the Azores in 1960–62. We have exchanged the same birthday card to each other for the past thirty years. We have used every ounce of space writing notes on the card but somehow find a new spot each year. We go visit them or they come here every other year. We toured Germany with them in 1986, and this year we are going on a river cruise from Bucharest to Budapest."

Reach Out to Those Who Are New

And don't forget, whether you are an introvert or an extrovert, put yourself in the new spouse's shoes. Remember what it's like to be brand new. Reach out and connect to spouses new to the military or new to your current base/post or your neighborhood.

Remember Shequita Gatlin who asked the question that prompted this new chapter? She left the book event that evening with two new friends because another spouse did reach out. After Shequita stood up to ask her question, Army spouse Yuri Nardi gave Shequita her phone number. "Yuri, her friend Caren and I went out afterwards," Shequita told us, "and we've gotten together since."

Resources

Girls Night Out, by Tamara Kreinin and Barbara Camens.

*Smart Networking (*formerly *Great Connections)* and their follow-on book, *Make Contacts Count,* by Anne Baber and Lynne Waymon (2002).

The Friendship Crisis: Finding, Making, and Keeping Friends When You're Not a Kid Anymore, by Marla Paul (2004).

Female Responses to Stress: Tend and Befriend, Not Fight or Flight, by Taylor, S. E., Klein, L.C., Lewis, B. P., Gruenewald, T. L., Gurung, R. A. R., & Updegraff, J. A. (Psychological Review, 107(3):41-429).

Fight Fat After Forty : The Revolutionary Three-Pronged Approach That Will Break Your Stress-Fat Cycle and Make You Healthy, Fit, and Trim for Life, by Pamela, MD Peeke (2000)

Chapter 4

If the Military Wanted You to Have a Spouse, They Would Have Issued You One

Relationship Resources and Ideas

Since strong support is important to your happiness in life, it would make sense that you would want strong support, a strong relationship with your spouse. Let's look at that.

The odds for any marriage in this country aren't great. Statistics indicate that nearly two-thirds of marriages end with divorce within forty years! That's the statistic for all marriages in the United States. And military marriages face much greater challenges than marriages in general. The stresses brought on by constant moves, repeated separations, long work hours, and frequent weekend work can wreak havoc with any relationship. It's a good idea to take proactive steps to work on your relationship and not take things for granted. Learn what works and what doesn't.

Find Something for Yourself and Strengthen Your Relationship

If you spend all your time taking care of everyone else and waiting for your spouse to come home, it's not a healthy relationship of two equal partners. When you look to your partner for your happiness and meaning in life, that's quite a burden for that partner. Not having interests and accomplishments of your own leads to low self-esteem.

As Michelle Weiner-Davis points out in the book *Divorce Busting,* "Unhappy marriages consist of unhappy people. If you are dissatisfied with your life, everything is colored by that fact. Little irritants become major crises. You've got a shorter fuse with the kids and you're more likely to respond rashly to your mate. Unless your life has definition and meaning without your mate, your relationship is doomed from the start."

Another challenge to a marriage occurs when one spouse doesn't have a support structure in place and he or she demands a lot of a partner. Looking to the partner for everything is especially problematic when that partner is deployed and can't be there. Depending on the partner exclusively is a problem when one person is working long hours, with a work schedule that is truly beyond an individual's control, as is often the case with the military.

Kathie recalls how she used to greet her husband in tears when he got home from work at Fort Rucker. After being by herself all day, she wanted to go out, while after being at work all day, he just wanted to stay home! She knows she isn't the first—or last—spouse to feel that way. That's why it's so important to have interests of your own as well. (We are talking

When you look to your partner for your happiness and meaning in life, that's quite a burden for that partner.

about healthy interests here, not going out clubbing and drinking with mixed groups when your spouses are away.) When you have interests of your own, you usually also have a group of people involved with those interests. You aren't isolated. Military communities provide many kinds of support structures. And don't forget, you can always start your own support structure in the form of a Dare to Dream team.

Of course, we've had people suggest when a person builds new interests, his or her spouse might be threatened by the way they are changing. We once wondered aloud how our message to spouses—about finding something for themselves—will work if they have a husband or wife who is totally unsupportive of them? When Holly's husband, Jack, heard that, he said, "Listen to what you are saying. If a spouse doesn't want [his or her] partner to be happy in life, there is something wrong with that relationship."

As Dr. Gottman, long-time relationship researcher, says, "Your partner's dreams are not a threat. They are the deep desires of someone you love."

Take Advantage of Marriage Enrichment Classes and Resources

A smart move for every military couple, before they find their relationship in trouble, is to proactively work on their relationship and to consider taking relationship courses. You don't have to reinvent the wheel here; learn from other people's experiences rather than having to make the same mistakes yourself. It's interesting how most parents read many books about pregnancy and childrearing to help them figure things out. But how many couples read up on relationship building?

Where can military couples turn for help in building a strong marriage? There are many resources offered within the military community. Family Life chaplains are being placed in many military communities. These are chaplains who have master's degrees in counseling psychology. Many places now offer marriage enrichment weekends, either through the unit or the post. In some cases, they are available from other services in the area. For example, a recent Fort Lewis, Washington, newspaper announcement provided information on Navy Marriage Enrichment retreats open to Army and Air Force couples as well (CREDO retreats are offered worldwide). As we've traveled around the globe presenting workshops for Marine Corps spouses, we've been very impressed with their Prevention and Relationship Enhancement Program (PREP). It's available free to all Marines and their spouses, and commands proactively encourage Marines to take part in these informative and fun marriage enrichment workshops (www.usmc-mccs.org).

Many military communities now offer workshops based on Gary Chapman's book, *The Five Love Languages.* As Chaplain Maj. Michael Strohm says, "The concept of this book is to fill the love tank of your loved one. Speak their love language. When their love tank is filled, they are now more able to attend to the needs of their partner." The book and workshops address the various ways that an individual perceives that he or she is loved. Their love language might be Words of Affirmation, Receiving Gifts, Physical Touch, Acts of Service, or Quality Time. What often causes discord in a relationship is when one person tries to show love in a language that their partner doesn't perceive as love.

Kathie sat in on another relationship class offered by Chaplain Maj. Thomas Cox at Fort Lewis's annual Parent University. She came out of it thinking, "Every military couple should be required to attend this session early in their marriage with refresher courses along the way!"

Chaplain Cox shared information based on the research of Dr. John M. Gottman. For more than thirty years, Dr. Gottman has studied what makes couples successful and unsuccessful, monitoring more than sixteen thousand couples in great depth. Dr. Gottman's book, *The Seven Principles for Making Marriage Work*, is based on his research and is full of great information and good exercises. It's worthwhile reading for any couple, troubled or not.

Some of the key points Cox made:

- Strengthen the friendship that is at the heart of any marriage. The more you know and understand about the other, the easier it is to keep connected when life swirls around you. Rest assured, in a military life, you'll face a lot of "swirling" times.
- Gottman's book has a lot of great exercises to help you get to know one another better. And part of that is knowing what your spouse does in the military.

- Ask questions, visit their place of work, take part in "Bring your family to work" days, and take advantage of "GI Jane/Jane Wayne" events. And make use of the "Military 101" type programs to learn their language (available through the Family Service Centers or on-line courses).
- When you don't make the effort to learn what your spouse does and vice versa, you end up living two very different and separate lives, which isn't great for any relationship.

Here's one fun way to get to know each other when your spouse is deployed—shared by a young woman in a Marine Corps spouse workshop. She types in "relationship quizzes" into Google. Thousands of fun quizzes come up. She chooses one to send to her husband. She answers the questions herself as well and they discuss their answers by email.

- Build a culture of appreciation between the two of you. One approach is to treat your spouse as well as you do your friends. "We already have the 'friend' skills," says Gottman, "After all, we don't talk to our friends in explosive, blaming ways. We have to learn to talk to our spouse like we talk to our friends." The words "please" and "thank you" aren't just words to use with strangers; we all need to hear them. We have to nurture fondness and admiration for each other, creating ways to say, "I love you." What's crucial here is that we learn how express love in the language that our partner understands.
- Turn toward rather than away from each other. Learn to communicate effectively and to build what Gottman calls a healthy emotional bank account. If you don't meet the emotional needs of your spouse, he or she will look to meet those needs elsewhere, and vice versa.
- Be aware of the Magic Ratio of five to one. Gottman has found that in successful relationships, there is a ratio of five positive interactions to every one negative one (since negative ones hold so much power).

Of course, it's challenging to even persuade military members to attend helpful workshops like these. The audience at Cox's workshops was mostly women. There were a few couples attending together. One young woman shared with Kathie that she and her husband were there trying to fix some pretty big problems that they had finally brought in to the chaplain's office, looking for help.

Even if you can get military members to overcome any false pride they might have about going to relationship classes, or overcome "Things are just fine; what do we need a class for?" thinking, with the rate of deployments and pace of training, where would they manage time during a workday? Now, if it were required as part of basic training or military family orientation programs, maybe it would be seen as a "normal" part of education. Then everyone who is married would come to think it is a normal part of being married—going to relationship classes along the way. The fact is that these are becoming much more common, offered by the units themselves as retreats for all unit members. Take advantage of them.

If no programs are available to you where you are located, use the books listed in the resource section of this chapter as a good starting point. One great idea is to each get a copy of Gottman's book and to work through it one chapter at a time, doing the exercises and discussing them with one another. You could even do that during a deployment via email or letters.

If your relationship needs help, counseling is available currently through Military One Source programs. You are eligible for six free confidential in-person counseling sessions, and that can be you, your spouse, or you as a couple. Be sure to check with your service family support centers to find out what is available—services change all the time as new needs are identified—things in this area might have changed by the time you read this, so be sure to ask.

But what if your spouse doesn't want to work on the relationship—doesn't want to read any of the books or go to workshops or for counseling? What can you do? Well, according to Weiner-Davis, long-time relationship counselor, "Relationships are such that if one person makes significant changes, the relationship must change . . . You can change your marriage by changing yourself."

Chaplain Cox agrees. "Generally speaking, when [spouses ask] their partner to read a book about marriage, there is another message being communicated. For example, from a female perspective they want their husband to read the book because they believe it will make their marriage better. A typical male hears the message: 'You're doing something wrong in this marriage and this book will help you.' It is more effective for one person to read a book that speaks to them and make changes themselves. Odds are the husband will begin to notice the change and may ask to learn more."

Learn from the Experience of Other Military Couples

Ask any spouse who has been married for a number of years what the secret to their success is and you'll get different answers. Here are some things we've heard from other military spouses.

- "Build on the strengths—don't magnify the weaknesses" is Holly's favorite relationship quote. Gottman's research backs that up. As he says, "Happily married couples aren't smarter, richer, or more psychologically astute than others. But in their day-to-day lives, they have hit upon a dynamic that keeps their negative thoughts and feelings about each other (which all couples have) from overwhelming their positive ones." After the honeymoon is over, it's all too common for couples to start focusing on what's missing in their mate and overlooking the fine qualities that are there. We often start taking our spouse's good qualities for granted.

- Start a "What I love about my spouse" list. Keep it on your computer (or in a journal) and keep it current. Once a month reread the list and relish what you've got! (Every now and then share that list with your spouse.) Or do what one Marine couple does. They share one item every evening before bed as in, "I love you today because . . ." listing one specific action or attribute that stood out that day.

- "Realize that sometimes in this military life," shares one Army spouse, "the feeling you get that your husband doesn't even know you exist—or at least doesn't seem to care—isn't true at all. Often it's the result of the extreme stress he is under in his job at the moment, where he simply doesn't have anything left to give." That can often happen in particularly high-stress positions such as First Sergeant, or Company Commander, Operations Officer, or Executive Officer, or during exceptionally challenging exercises or inspections. "Don't worry," Amy adds, "he'll be back to being himself as he moves on to a less demanding position."

- Recognize and plan for the stresses that every move can put on a relationship. As long-time Army spouse Christina Clarkson says, "We go to great lengths to find out about schools, housing, jobs, etc. when we move. But how many people give any thought to how it will affect the marriage? With all the millions of details to deal with, we don't usually take much time to find ways to pamper our relationship as husband and wife." As she points out, moving is listed as one of the most stressful life events. In fact, some military spouses have even named this challenge "cardboard box poisoning." Maybe we all need to add to our moving "to-do" list some things specifically for us as a couple: make dinner reservations as soon as possible after arriving at the new location; schedule a surprise for one another (massage, flowers, etc.); agree on what is off limits, in other words no arguing over small things, no yelling unless the house is on fire, and so on.

- Take advantage of a powerful tool that Navy spouse Sherrie learned from a *Reader's Digest* article many years ago. A marriage counselor interviewed for the article mentioned a magic question that can change a relationship for the better. The question to ask yourself on a regular basis is, "What would it be like to be married to me?" As Sherrie reports, she reads that question once a month. "It's so easy to focus on what my husband is doing wrong, or not doing. That question stops me short each time as I acknowledge lapses in my own behavior. It makes me change—at least for a while anyway—which is why I read it every month!"

- Recognize that the reasons behind your spouse's actions may be different than you think. Capt. Rich Brown, Ph.D., a former Navy officer, wrote the book *Engineers in Love . . . Unlocking the Heart of the Technical Male.* As he says, "I use the term engineer, but the messages hold for other professions that deal with the world of logic, structure and rules, such as the military." He has three simple things to teach husbands: "Talk to your wife. Make room for your kids. Take care of yourself. The 'what to do' is simple—it is the doing of it that is awkward, especially at first." That's why many men tend to head to work even when they don't have to. They know how to do work; it can seem easier than the complicated relationship challenges at home. Realize that some men will cover *scared* with *angry*. "Men often use anger to cover their fear of not being able to fix the problem," says Rich. Just knowing that can change how you approach communications and interactions when anger shows up.

- Cultivate interests in common with your spouse. Martha, an Air Force spouse, suggests that although it's important to have something you do for yourself, especially critical during deployments, it's also important that you cultivate interests in common with your spouse. "It's important that you spend some of your recreational time doing things as a couple," she stresses, "rather than spending all your together time doing chores or discussing the children or in separate pursuits." Here's a great idea from Della Elzie, a Marine spouse and mother of three. With each new assignment, she and her husband take on one new activity they haven't done before. "We scuba'd in Cuba, tried golf in Hawaii, and ran a marathon together in Virginia."

- Recognize the importance of fun. Terry Sovinski, family and marriage counselor in Vilseck, Germany, says many times couples' problems are the result of lack of shared fun. They just can't remember the last time they had fun together as a couple. If you fall into this category, be sure to do the Simple Joys exercise in chapter 6 with your spouse. Start adding in the things that you both enjoy—things that are fun for both of you. And see what a difference that makes in your relationship.

- Schedule regular date nights with your spouse when they aren't deployed. "It seems crazy that you have to consciously schedule in time to be together alone," added one wife, "but that's reality. If you don't schedule it in your calendars, it doesn't happen!" Gottman's research backs this up. His recommendation is to have a weekly date with your spouse. Chaplain

Cox modified that for military during the workshop. "Of course, that would be ideal, but with the OPTEMPO today, once a month might be more realistic." And that's when they aren't deployed of course. With deployments so common now, date nights when spouses are here are even more crucial. He did stress the importance of choosing what you do on a date. Going to a movie doesn't really count here because it means you don't get to talk with each other. Unless of course you go to a movie for the stress release of laughing together at a comedy and then take time for coffee and conversation after the show. Find a way to spend time together to talk about life, not about finances or chores or your children.

Here are date-night ideas from other military spouses.

- One couple has a date on the twenty-seventh of every month since their wedding was on the twenty-seventh. It's easy to remember and they take turns in planning what they do on the date.
- Marine spouse Kathleen Schmidt and her husband occasionally have what they call "teen date" nights. "We do what you used to do as a teen to have fun together," she says. "We go for ice cream and a walk on the beach, take sticky photos in those 'small photo booths,' make out on the Ferris Wheel, and we act goofy and laugh, laugh, laugh."
- When your children are old enough, involve them. Holly has her twins help her set the mood for mom and dad's date night at home by setting the table with candles and flowers and choosing the music. Her children get pizza and a video in the family room so Holly and Jack can have time talking together alone.
- Marine spouse Cindy Garland always creates a "Date Night Co-op" wherever they live so couples get date nights out without the expense of baby sitters. "We look for two other families with children of similar ages as our own," she explains. The first Friday of the month all the kids go to one house where the parents provide inexpensive dinner and games, while the other two couples get a date night. That rotates from house to house with the fourth Friday reserved as family night for all of them.

Access Additional Relationship Resources at Reunion Time

Kathie's mother-in-law, Naomi, always said only half-jokingly, "You two never have time to get tired of each other—you're always saying hello or goodbye." There may be some truth to that when we are talking about short TDY trips—the old saying, "Absence makes the heart grow fonder." That may not be as true for long separations.

Reunions after deployments are challenging, no matter how joyful and romantic they seem at first. Expect that, plan for it, and take advantage of the resources and information (brochures, workshops) provided by the services addressing those times. With the new face of deployments during the Iraq war and the increased possibility of Post Traumatic Stress Disorder, reunions become even more challenging. The reality is that the services don't yet have enough research about how best to help families deal with the new challenges. So even if you've been through one reunion and one reunion workshop, don't assume that every future reunion will be the same. There is a big difference in the issues you face during a reunion for a generally safe peacekeeping deployment in Kosovo versus a reunion with a soldier who has been through combat in Iraq. The reunion workshops provided by the services will improve as they learn more about what to expect and what can help with this challenging transition. This is one situation where you really don't want to figure this out by yourself.

Resources

Divorce Busting: A Revolutionary and Rapid Program for Staying Together, by Michelle Weiner-Davis (1992).

Engineers in Love . . . Unlocking the Heart of the Technical Male, by Capt. Rich Brown, Ph.D. (2004), www.engineersinlove.com or captdrb@tampa bay.rr.com.

His Needs, Her Needs: Building an Affair-Proof Marriage, by Willard E. Harley, Jr. (2001).

The Five Love Languages: How to Express Heartfelt Commitment to Your Mate, by Gary Chapman (1995).

The Seven Principles for Making Marriage Work, by John Gottman, Ph.D., with Nan Silver. Gottman's website (www.gottman.com) has self-help tips, some good relationship quizzes, and other resources.

Chapter 5

Faith, Hope, and Gratitude

Essentials to Your Overall Happiness in Life

When we are able to develop a strong spiritual faith during peaceful times, it will be there to support and sustain us through times of crisis. People who tap into their spiritual side have a greater life satisfaction than those who don't.

There aren't very many other lifestyles as challenging as the military—especially in the midst of terrorism and war. As military spouses when we allow our peace of mind to be affected by the external happenings of the world, it is almost impossible to quiet our souls and connect our hearts with our heads so we can nurture our spiritual health and grow. Finding some practice that allows us to quiet our minds and grow spiritually can help us get away from the constant thoughts of worry and fear, and from the litany of things we still have to do. Having a strong faith and spiritual health helps to remind us that even in times of turmoil there is a place we can go for peace, a peace we can always rely on.

Finding your spiritual center and developing your faith is an internal event, not an external one. This means slowing down and listening within for guidance.

Think of Glenda the Good Witch as she said to Dorothy in the Wizard of Oz, "You've always had the power." Everyone owns a pair of ruby slippers, whether you know it or not. It is up to you to click your heels and find your way back home to yourself, to your center. We are all different in our beliefs, in our faiths, in our paths back home.

Faith is defined as the firm belief in something for which there is no proof—a belief in something greater than yourself. Religions have long promised those who are faithful rewards of inner peace, comfort, and joy and a sense of well-being. A belief in something greater than yourself provides you with a sense of hope, optimism, and purpose. Recently, more and more scientific research has been published on the beneficial relationship between religion and health and happiness. The research does not point to any specific religion—simply the belief in something greater than ourselves.

Harold G. Koenig, MD, is the co-director of the Center for Spirituality, Theology, and Health at Duke University Medical Center, and has published extensively in the fields of mental health, geriatrics, and religion with more than thirty books in print or in preparation. He has been diligent in his field documenting the faith-medical initiative, which promotes the holistic approach of body, mind, and spirit in healing.

In the book, *Handbook of Religion and Health,* Dr. Koenig along with other researchers examined twelve hundred separate research studies conducted over the past century (1900–2000). Their work is called the most comprehensive book of its kind ever assembled. It reviews and discusses the extensive research on the relationship between religion and a variety of mental and physical health outcomes.

The research in this book reveals individuals of faith and who are involved in religious activities are more likely to experience:

- well-being, happiness, and life satisfaction,
- hope and optimism,
- purpose and meaning in life,
- higher self-esteem,
- adaptation to bereavement,
- greater social support and less loneliness,
- lower rates of depression and faster recovery from depression,
- less anxiety,
- less psychosis and fewer psychotic tendencies,
- lower rates of alcohol and drug use or abuse,
- less delinquency and criminal activity, and
- greater marital stability and satisfaction.

How can we strengthen our spiritual health in today's fast-paced challenging military lifestyle? It's a lifestyle that leaves very little room for reflection time. When we interviewed military spouses and asked them to share ways in which they were able to develop their faith and spiritual heath they provided us with the following list of ideas:

Daily Prayer, Weekly Service, Bible Study, and Reading Inspirational Devotionals.

Regardless of the precise nature of its origins, prayer has long been a feature of virtually every living religion, from Christianity to Buddhism. Prayer is an act of communion with God, such as in devotion, confession, praise, or thanksgiving. Prayer may be oral or mental, occasional or constant, secret or social.

Carolyn, a Marine spouse, shares these thoughts from a recent deployment, "The long months of the deployment were the most difficult times in my life. When someone goes through times like this you have to have something to hang on to in order to get to the next day—sometimes through the next hour. The only thing I could always count on being there was my faith. It's amazing how close you can become to your God when you feel absolutely alone."

Cathy Sterling, an Army spouse, shares this great idea on how to create a way to spend more time in prayer. "In the book *Practical Prayer* Anne Tanner suggests making physical and mental space for God within your home. Find a space where you can be in silence, relax, and be comfortable. At the bazaar last fall, I saw a church kneeler (Prie-dieu) in one of the antique booths and was intrigued, thinking that might help me focus better in my prayer life. There is something about kneeling in prayer in church that I always find comforting and focusing. Someone else bought the kneeler before I decided I really wanted it, so I've been wanting one ever since. Two of my friends went to a flea market and surprised me with one the other day. It is beautiful and is very inviting and comfortable to kneel at. I put it in my bedroom and see it as I wake up every morning and go to sleep at night, so of course, it invites me to come kneel and say some prayers."

In addition to reading the Bible, Holly likes to turn to inspirational devotionals to inspire her spiritual growth. One book of devotionals for military spouses she highly recommends is *Medals Above My Heart*, written by two military spouses, Brenda Pace and Carol McGlothlin. Most military communities offer ways to enjoy the treasures of fellowship, religious study, and spiritual growth through the community's chaplain offices. You'll find a myriad of activities, from church services and Sunday school to weekly Protestant Women of the Church (PWOC) Bible studies to Catholic Women of the Church (CWOC) to Bible studies. All it takes is for you to reach out to seek these opportunities for spiritual growth.

Journaling

While many people use blogs or computer programs to record their thoughts, putting pen to paper and "journaling" can be a powerful life tool toward self-awareness and spiritual growth. Journaling is a nonjudgmental and all-accepting friend. As a matter of fact, it is possibly the cheapest therapy you will ever get.

There is increasing evidence to support the notion that journaling has a positive impact on physical well-being. James Pennebaker, a psychologist and researcher from University of Texas at Austin, contends that regular journaling strengthens the immune cells. According to Pennebaker, writing about stressful events helps you come to terms with them, thus reducing the impact of those stressors on your physical health.

Consider the following benefits of journaling noted by James Pennebaker and Maud Purcell, LCSW, CEAP, a psychotherapist and researcher.

- Journaling helps to clarify your thoughts and feelings: Do you ever seem all jumbled up inside, unsure of what you want or feel? Taking a few minutes to jot down your thoughts and emotions (no editing!) will quickly get you in touch with your internal self.
- Journaling assists you in knowing yourself better. By writing routinely you will get to know what makes you feel happy and confident. You will also become clear about situations and people who are toxic for you— important information for your emotional well-being.
- Journaling reduces stress. Writing about stressful events helps you come to terms with them, allowing you to feel calmer and better able to stay in the present.
- Journaling solves problems more effectively. Typically we problem solve from a left-brained, analytical perspective. But sometimes the answer can only be found by engaging right-brained creativity and intuition. Writing unlocks these other capabilities, and affords the opportunity for unexpected solutions to seemingly unsolvable problems.
- Journaling assists in resolving disagreements with others. Writing about misunderstandings rather than stewing over them will help you to understand another's point of view. And you may come up with a sensible resolution to conflict.

Kathie is one who has journaled for years and can't imagine figuring out her life without it. "I read back over my journals once a year on my birthday—it's my gift to myself. I often discover good decisions I made but never implemented so I can then choose to make the change. I've also learned the power in working things through in my journal before sending off an angry email response or telephone call." She uses her journal to capture random thoughts as well as to write out her responses to self-exploration exercises—the kind that help to figure out who you are and what's most important to you.

Daily Meditation and/or Yoga or Tai Chi

Learning to be still is one of the most valuable ways to nurture your soul. Start your meditation by repeating a mantra or prayer to help settle your busy mind. Whether it's something like "Om" or "Let go, let God," a mantra can quiet that nonstop "Monkey Mind" many of us have, spinning always. Then spend time in silence gently using your breath to recenter yourself when your mind gets active again. For some people, using chanting tapes or CDs helps in quieting the mind and staying focused. Kathie's current favorite is *Embrace* by Deva Premal, but it's important to find one that speaks to you. For others focusing on a candle in complete silence works best.

Another possibility for quieting and centering is practicing yoga. "Legs Up the Wall" is one of our favorite quieting poses. We do it every time we travel or after standing for long periods of time presenting our seminars. We also do it many evenings at home to quiet ourselves after a hectic day.

The pose is simple, requires no equipment, and can take as little as five to ten minutes (although fifteen minutes is heaven). Here are a few variations. You'll figure out which feels best for your body.

"Legs Up the Wall"

Classic Variation: Lie on the floor next to a wall, slide your bottom up against the wall, swing your legs up the wall with your back resting on the floor and your arms lying out by your side, palms up. Close your eyes and just let your body relax. This allows you to reverse gravity a bit. It takes all the tension out of your neck, shoulders, and back areas where many of us carry the weight of the world all day.

A nice addition is to use an eye pillow over your eyes. These are small pillows filled with buck seed or rice and aromatherapy (like lavender) to add to your relaxation. The weight of the pillow causes your eye muscles to totally relax. By blocking out the light you relax even more. Just zone out for a while. Let your thoughts and worries go for now.

Floor Variation: Lie flat on the floor (either with carpeting or on a towel for padding.) Place your feet flat on the floor with your knees bent. Relax. To add to the relaxation, put your hands on your knees and gently rotate your knees in a circular motion, first in one direction and then the other. What you are doing is massaging you lower back, where a lot of us carry extra tension.

Try either of these and see if it doesn't make a big difference. You'll reduce your stress; quiet your mind, return to your center.

Note to parents: One of the greatest gifts you can give your children is to teach them how to listen within for guidance. Our children's lives today are filled with busyness. Showing them the importance of stopping and being quiet is an invaluable lesson. Let them know that even in times of turmoil there is a place they can go for peace, a peace they can always rely on.

Holly desperately wanted to find a way to incorporate yoga and quiet time into her daily activities and wanted to teach its value to her twins when they were preschoolers. However she found sitting in most yoga poses was not working because her twins kept fidgeting. She found Legs Up the Wall to be an excellent pose to get the children involved in because she could have one on each side of her and their fingertips would touch each other. This soft touch was a gentle reminder to each child to lie quietly. The key is to put one child on each side, not next to one another.

They started out being "quiet" for the length of a certain familiar song and the time would increase with each successive day. As they got better with being "quiet" they started to ask what they were supposed to think about when they were quiet. Holly encouraged them to "tell God about all the wonderful things in your life and just tell God about your day." It got to the point where her children started asking, "When do we get to have time to do Legs Up the Wall?"

Cultivate Quiet Time:
Find Time for Self-Reflection in Simple Activities

When the mind is engaged in simple daily activities that are effortless for you, you are better able to connect with your spiritual center.

Nancy Boatner, an Army spouse, finds her "quiet time" while she vacuums! When we first heard that she vacuumed her house twice a day, we admit to thinking immediately that she's a bit obsessive, but then we talked with Nancy and found out her secret of the vacuum.

"Hey, I have three young children at home and a husband who is away," she told us many years ago. "How much 'me' time do you think I get? When I'm vacuuming, the children know they can't bother me, and they have to play until I am done." Vacuuming gave her time to let her thoughts flow, to turn off the many questions and demands of her young children, to just "be" for a time. The fact that she ended up with a clean house was icing on the cake. Now that we know Nancy's secret we've been sharing it with other moms over the years. Just think of the benefits of vacuuming   exercise, alone time, and a clean floor. Pretty smart, huh?

Linda Beougher plays the harp. She's found that if she plays the harp, especially favorites such as "Somewhere Over the Rainbow" as her girls are falling asleep, they sleep better, and she calms her mind at the same time.

Cathy Sterling is a weaver. She sets up her loom in whatever quarters they get, even if the only space is in the middle of the living room. When she's weaving, she enters a state of flow, letting all the other stuff go for that time.

Army spouse Monica Dixon has a similar experience when she quilts.

For you it might be knitting, gardening, scrap booking or woodwork, sewing, or bread making. Whatever works for you, carve out quiet time to get to your core. The centering and quieting that results from these activities will help carry you through the stressful, chaotic times.

Time in Nature

Enjoying nature, walking or hiking, watching a glorious sunset or sunrise, noticing the celestial rays shine through the trees in the woods, as well as listening to the waves of the ocean are all ways to stop and take stock in the power of the universe—and to step away from the busyness of daily life to get quiet within.

Deep Conversations with Friends

We've already spent time in chapter 3 on the importance of having friends and how to make friends. Deep conversations with friends that get past the superficial into heartfelt feelings about life help many military spouses dig deeper into their own faith. These types of conversations can help to solidify your own beliefs just by having the opportunity to talk about why you believe what you believe and to understand where misconceptions and misunderstanding begin. You don't have to get philosophical. Just start by asking a friend to share their spiritual beliefs as well as ways they have found to strengthen their spiritual health.

When you allow yourself to get away from the constant thoughts of worry and fear, and from the litany of things you still have to do, you will be amazed at the strength and knowledge you already have within—you may not have ever tapped into it before. Developing a strong sense of faith and spiritual health during peaceful times will support and sustain you through times of crisis.

The Importance of Gratitude—And the Lesson of the Rainbow Glasses

Our signature prop in our workshops is a pair of colorful rainbow glasses. When you look through these glasses everything you look at is surrounded by rainbows, even negative, complaining people. Seeing rainbows changes our attitudes. The rainbow glasses are a fun, colorful, playful reminder for all of us to look for the good in other people and in situations.

Negative things are going to happen to you in life—guaranteed. When something negative happens, you have two choices. You can do what Kathie used to do which was focus on the negative, wallow in the negative, and obsess about the negative. When you do that, we guarantee that your situation will become more negative, you'll become more negative, and what's even worse, you'll attract negative people to you.

The opposite is also true. When something negative happens you can choose instead to look for the good. It may be that it's a tiny, tiny nugget of good or of value, but just the fact that you are looking for the positive necessarily shifts your focus out of the negative. If you choose to do that consciously, consistently, we guarantee that you'll become more positive, your life will become more positive, and what's really wonderful is that you'll attract other positive people to you. You'll change your overall experience of life.

Part of that choice of joy and looking for the good includes giving gratitude for what you already have. A study by the University of California–Davis, (Emmons and McCullough 2003), found that people who wrote down five things for which they were grateful in weekly or daily journals were not only more joyful, they were healthier, less stressed, more optimistic, and more likely to help others.

Stacy Miller, an Army spouse, wrote to us and said gratitude is a value she holds dear. "It's important to me that I show gratitude for the many blessings that I have and receive." As military spouses, especially when we deal with deployments, it's easy to focus on the stress and negatives. After all, they are real—and foremost in our minds.

While Stacy's husband was deployed she chose to focus on the good. One of those focal points was gratitude for the many friends and neighbors who helped her make it through that tough time.

"When my husband returned, I felt like I needed to do something for everyone who helped me by raking leaves, watching my children, making us dinner, etc.," Stacy explained. "I decided to have a *How can you expect any more blessings in your life if you aren't grateful for what you've already been given?* Valentine's Day cookie social. It's kind of like a cookie exchange, except I did all the baking. It was a great opportunity to thank people again—and for my husband to thank people for helping take care of us during his absence."

Taking the time to switch our focus to what we are grateful for can make a difference in how we experience and approach our situations.

Your choice of focus can affect your children as well. After hearing Dr. James Crupi speak at an Army Morale, Welfare, and Recreation conference, Kathie has been sharing something he said that really struck her. "If you go home at night and complain about change, you will raise kids who fear change. If you sit around the dinner table and everything is negative, you will raise kids who are negative." Try starting your dinner conversations with the question,

"What's one good—or funny—thing that happened to you today?" rather than diving into the more common litany of complaints.

Doris Burns, an Army Reserve spouse, can attest to the power of this idea. "I wanted to tell you that we've been using the 'what's one good thing' at supper time. Clara (age five at the time) loves it! It does help in keeping the conversation positive. Dave sometimes has difficulty being positive after a challenging day at work, but this helps. Now, Clara will actually start the conversation by asking us, 'What's one good thing that happened to you today?' It's pretty cute—and positive!"

Here's one simple example of how your focus and attitude can change a negative experience. Joan is an Army spouse who wrote us this card after attending one of our workshops: "I attended your seminar last week and just wanted to thank you and share a quick story that happened as a result of what I learned from you two. I've just moved here and since my husband is deployed, I get to do this move all by myself. So I'm sitting in the midst of these boxes, feeling quite angry. I opened one box and all these pictures fell out all over the place. Normally, I'd have said a few choice words, stuffed them into a folder and plodded on. Instead I took your advice from the seminar to heart and savored the moment. I called the kids down and we spent an hour tripping down memory lane. It put us all into a better mood and I even got them to help me do some more unpacking—hoping to find more treasures like the photos. Thanks for a great day and a different perspective on boxes!"

Holly's Story

I had heard about Grateful Journals from friends, watching Oprah, and reading books. I started my own when I began reading Sarah Ban Breathnach's book, Simple Abundance. *Writing in my Grateful Journal helped me come up with my new mantra "Focus on the Good Road."*

We all have good roads and bad roads to travel on in life. It's a guarantee of life. The funny thing about life is the good and bad roads run parallel with each other. Sometimes the bad road seems a bit wider and longer than the good road, but nonetheless, the good road is always running alongside the bad road. We just have to turn our heads and notice all the good.

Identifying all the things I am grateful for honestly does make me see more clearly how wonderful my life really is overall. I took this approach one step further during a time when the twins were preschoolers and daddy was gone again for long periods of time.

Sound familiar to anyone? I began individual Grateful Journals with each child. We purchased colorful journals and each night before they went to bed I spent time with each child and wrote in their journal what they were grateful for that day. Some of the entries were simple: "I am grateful for the ice cream we ate tonight." Others were lengthy entries about all the fun things they did that day.

Doing this every night allowed us to end the day on a positive note. I can't explain how it happened, but the empty feelings and anxieties we all were experiencing while daddy was away seemed to fade. The children slept better. I slept better knowing my children did have things to be grateful for and their little lives were filled with joy even though daddy was far away being a soldier. I also felt better as a mother that I was helping my children early in their lives to turn their heads and Focus on the Good Road.

We have both kept gratitude journals for many years now. We don't record in them daily anymore because we now have the habit of reviewing what we're grateful for when we're falling asleep at night. But we find ourselves turning to our gratitude journals every couple of months if we are going through a bit of a slump. Reading through the list and adding to it puts us right back into a feeling of abundance. You can start with one of these methods.

Method One: Sit down and write down one hundred things you are grateful for. Small and large. Even if you don't reach one hundred, just working toward that will throw you into that "wallowing in abundance" mode.

Method Two: Make a list of ten things for which you are grateful. Each evening for thirty days, read the list and add one more. By the end of thirty days you'll be living in abundance thinking.

As one Marine spouse suggested in a recent workshop, "For some people scrap booking is like keeping a gratitude journal as you make collages and collections of all these positive memories in your life."

One last thing about gratitude. As military spouses we are fortunate to get perspective as we move around and live and travel in different places. We are often more aware than many Americans of living conditions in other countries as we read about and watch on television reports of the conditions of the areas of the world our spouses deploy to. We know that we live in one of the most (if not *the* most) abundant places in the world. It's helpful to remind ourselves of that on a regular basis.

Resources

Handbook of Religion and Health, by Harold G. Koenig, MD, Michael E. McCullough, and David B. Larson (2001).

Medals Above My Heart, by Brenda Pace and Carol McGlothlin (2004).

Practical Prayer, by Anne Tanner (2002).

The Woman's Book of Yoga and Health: A Lifelong Guide to Wellness, by Linda Sparrowe with Patricia Walden (2002).

Writing to Heal: A Guided Journal for Recovering from Trauma and Emotional Upheaval, by Pennebaker, J.W. (2004).

Counting blessings versus burdens: Experimental studies of gratitude and subjective well-being in daily life, by Emmons, R.A., & McCullough, M.E. (2003). Journal of Personality and Social Psychology, 84, 377-389.

Chapter 6

Simple Joys . . . and Energy for Life!

How to Have the Energy to Go for Your Dreams

One Simple Exercise—For Joy and Energy

Simple joys can bring us happiness— and energy. Could you use a bit more energy in life? Before we go into this subject, do this simple exercise. Pull out your journal or a piece of paper and get your pen ready. Think of the things you do for fun, and write down as many as you can and as fast as you can. You might have to think, "If I only had the time to have fun, I would; or if I only allowed myself to have fun, I would . . . . For example, one of us loves to kayak with her husband, watch movies, and garden. The other loves to take hot baths, get manicures, and travel any place! So take a moment and make your list . . . write as many things as you can think of as fast as you can.

The research for this came from *You Don't Have to Go Home from Work Exhausted,* by Ann McGee-Cooper, Ph.D., and her colleagues out of Dallas. This is a book we highly recommend, whether you work outside the home or not (we think stay-at-home moms need more energy than anyone!). It is full of great ideas of ways to increase your daily energy. One thing the authors discovered was that most busy adults, when asked, "What do you do for fun?" usually come up with ten to fifteen items before running out of ideas.

Researchers did this with ten-year-olds. Ten-year-olds easily came up with fifty-five items before running out of ideas! We had a fourteen-year-old boy in one of our sessions and he came up with thirty-two items, so we think there's a pattern here, a transition that takes place, as we grow older.

So what does that say to us as adults? The responses we get from audience members include:

- "It means we are boring."
- "We have forgotten how to have fun."
- "We don't have time; we have too many responsibilities."

There are two common problems for most adults.

- Some of us actually have forgotten what is fun. We are so caught up in our work and chores and responsibilities that we have forgotten to have fun.
- Many of us don't allow ourselves to have fun. We say things like, "I'd really like to do that, but I should do the laundry." Or, "I'd really like to do that, but I should mow the lawn." Or, "I'd really like to do that, but . . ."

There's another problem for us as busy adults. Look back at your list and circle items that would take only five to ten minutes to do and enjoy. When we ask audience members how many have the majority of their items circled, we rarely get hands raised. This is also typical of most busy adults. When asked what they do for fun most adults come up with items that take an hour or longer or a half day or longer to do.

Now think about your typical day. When you have free time in your busy day, does it come in big chunks of time of one hour or longer or a half day or longer? For most of us any free time we have comes in five minutes here, ten minutes there, even more so during deployments.

If you have short breaks in your busy day and you don't know what's fun for you to do to fill them with, what do you fill them with instead? Well, some of us complain to neighbors or coworkers. We join the "Ain't it Awful" club. Some of us—and we know this because we used to do this—make lists of things we still have to do. Right? And worry about them, which is not a very energizing break.

The fact is if you take a five- or ten-minute break and fill it with something that is *not* fun for you, you are going to return to your work or chores with less energy and joy. Research shows that if instead you fill your short break with things you enjoy doing, you will return to your work and your chores with more energy. If you fill your break with something that is playful or that makes you laugh, you also come back with more creativity and problem-solving ability.

Here are ways to increase your list of short fun items:

1. Share it with other people. When you hear other's ideas you'll hear things that you enjoy too but you just forgot. You can add those to your list. You may also hear things you just never would have thought of. We were in Heidelberg,

Germany, at a conference for drug and alcohol counselors sharing ideas. A gentleman sitting in the front row quickly raised his hand to say, "The first thing I thought of and wrote down was to *Jump up and down.*" We were thankful we weren't having our session videotaped that day, because we know our faces gave away what we were thinking. "Oh . . . really . . . that's nice; that's . . . interesting."

But then we decided to try it out, and discovered he was right! Since then we've done this with every audience. We get them jumping up and down. And everyone agrees. It raises your energy. Most folks can't help but laugh, so your joy and creativity rise as well.

Fill your break with something that is playful or that makes you laugh, return to your work with more creativity and more problem-solving ability.

Lest you think this idea is silly, read the email we received from one Army spouse a few months after our workshop in Vilseck, Germany: "When you told us the jump up and down story, I didn't take it seriously. How could I jump up and down in the middle of a store? But the other day in my kickboxing class, the instructor told us to do something new. She wanted us to do full jumps, arms in the air and all the way back to the ground. She suggested we try for two minutes. I don't think we even got to thirty seconds before the whole class was incapacitated because we were laughing so hard. That was the most fun class we ever had, just because we '*jumped up and down.*' I think I might be doing it a little more often—at home anyway. Thanks, Jennifer Campbell."

Here are short, simple joys that other spouses have mentioned:

- Take a quick walk outside. A ten-minute walk increases your energy for one full hour. (And best of all, researchers at Northern Arizona University found that just ten minutes of exercise is all it takes to improve overall mood!)
- Pet your dog or cat.
- Use the Tingler (a fun head massager available through www.Isabell acatalog.com and other sources).
- Write a postcard to a friend. You have the joy of thinking about them and they have the joy in receiving a note from you.
- Sing out loud or dance around the room.

2. Break longer items into smaller ones. Look at those things that take longer and figure out what piece of that activity you could do in five to ten minutes. For example, how could you find a way to enjoy golfing in five to ten minutes? You could putt, you could practice your swing (with or without a club), and you could look through a golf magazine or call a friend to schedule a tee time. Or you could close your eyes, talk yourself into relaxation and then visualize yourself playing golf on a gorgeous day on your favorite course. Any one of those things would be a more energizing break than worrying or complaining.

3. Go to the toy store with yourself in mind. (We're talking about Toys 'R' Us or Wal-Mart or the Exchange toy section here.) Don't think about your kids or nieces and nephews or grandkids, but with just you in mind. Here's what you'll find.

You will find toys that you loved as a kid. For example, Slinky toys turned sixty a few years ago. Etch-a-Sketches™ are still around. You'll also find new fun toys that didn't exist when you were little. There is a saying: You don't stop playing because you grow old. You grow old because you stop playing! And even the business guru Tom Peters says, "An office without a toy is like computer without software." We all need play and laughter and fun in our lives.

Remember, when you fill your short breaks with things you enjoy doing, you return to your work and your chores with more energy. In addition, if you fill your break with something that is playful or that makes you laugh, you also come back with more creativity and problem-solving ability. Let's face it, during a deployment especially, if you are acting as a single parent handling all the chores, all you have time for are short simple joys. You need all the energy and problem-solving ability you can get, so consciously add in fun things. And an important added note here about deployments. We know how natural it is to think, "How can I do fun things even in small doses when my spouse is in danger?" The fact of the matter is that during deployments especially, you have to incorporate these small joys, for your energy and for your sanity!

Doing this exercise as a group or family is also a great idea. We've seen this successfully done in Family Readiness Group meetings, Key Volunteer groups, clubs and office meetings, as well as within families. Once you understand this concept of filling your day with simple joys, you will see that it is the accumulation of these simple joys that brings you that sense of overall happiness with life.

By the way, don't forget to use the items on your list that take an hour or longer. Compare lists with those of your spouse and your children. Schedule in things you enjoy doing together on a regular basis. If we don't plan and schedule these things in, they often don't happen.

It's important for your relationship to consciously add fun in. As Terry Sovinski, a family counselor in Vilseck, Germany, told a group of military spouses during a Family Readiness Group orientation, one of the main things he sees in couples that are in trouble is a lack of shared fun. We come together through activities we enjoy doing together. You've heard the saying, "No one on their death bed ever said, I wish I spent more time at the office." Well, we think no one on her deathbed ever said, "Boy I wish I'd kept a cleaner house," or "Boy, I wish I'd watched more television." Make time for fun in your life. Plan for it. You'll increase your joy—and your energy. The research proves it.

Holly's Story

My hardest lesson: Letting Go! *Enjoying the moments!*

You would think someone as playful as me would have fun playing with my children each day. Sadly, not so. I would feel the weight of daily responsibilities, managing a home, community involvement, disciplining, and work deadlines always hanging over me. It made me feel stressed and unhappy with my role as a parent. I was well aware of the fact that the lives of my children were flying by and I wanted to cherish those times, but it seemed I often let the other responsibilities take over. The "joy of parenting" just wasn't there for me.

The Wall Street Journal *had a regular column called "A Balanced Life" in which a controversial discussion between working mothers and nonworking mothers arose. (Don't you think "nonworking mothers" is an oxymoron?) One letter hit home."One of the key things overlooked in this 'battle' is that the success of the stay-at-home mom is perhaps best measured by how* little *she accomplishes, not how much. When she is truly connecting with her child/children, she is not doing laundry, dishes, cooking, yard work, driving, etc. (and I add, volunteer work) She is doing nothing except hanging out and being with her kids. This requires a tremendous mental shift from her former career where success meant getting things done. Success with kids means* not *getting things done, except the bare minimum, because only when you are hanging out in the hammock, watching the leaves fall . . . are you giving them the absolute, undivided attention they crave. Most people have not made this mental shift."*

I certainly fell into this category, as I was notorious for making "to do" lists and expecting to get the majority of the items done. I was continually disappointed at the end the day when I only accomplished one or two things on my list. Why did I continue to punish myself like this? Why couldn't I learn to just let go and enjoy this time with my children, let alone take time to care for myself?

Some people have an easier time letting go than others. My mental shift is a work in progress. One step I took toward letting go was to make a "to-do" list with my children at breakfast or the night before. I actually wrote the items or the children drew pictures of what we were going to do that day. Each child got to put down what she or he wanted to include. At the time we started this, my twins were four years old and 99.9 percent of their items included mommy playing with them. (For example, play dolls with mommy; play cars with mommy; go to the park with mommy.) They wanted my individual and undivided attention. Doesn't every child? Completing this list with the children helped them understand there are things mommy wanted to get done that day and it was also a visible reminder for me to stop and play with each child. As their mother, this is exactly what I wanted to be doing—every day! Furthermore, it helped them know mommy was going to spend time with them that day. After we completed an item on the list we got to cross it off. The feeling of accomplishment makes me feel like I am doing a good job.

One particular morning my daughter's item was to pick dandelions with mommy, lie on the grass, and watch the clouds together. Children are so wise— if you just listen. They understand the concept of Simple Joys! My daughter certainly does!

So, simple joys can bring you energy as well as happiness. We want to share other ways to increase your energy and decrease your stress. Why? Because the following is a common response we get to the concept of "following your dreams."

"Go for my dreams?" people say. "I wish I could, but I can hardly get myself out of bed in the morning. By the end of the day, I'm dragging. About all I can manage is to slump in front of the television to relax a bit, get to bed, and start all over again the next day. I don't have any energy left to get going on something new, especially something as big as my dreams!"

Sound familiar? We hear this all the time. So, before we get into the how-to of happiness, let's look at how to increase your energy on a regular basis. If you are tired and running on empty, the last thing you will do is move forward toward your dreams. You won't even have the energy to get excited about the idea! You must address self-care first.

When Holly was the new mom of twins and dealing with her husband's deployment, she was low on energy herself. Giving all her energy to take care of her children and her community, she would often say, "If I can comb my hair and brush my teeth in the same day—it's a good day." That is all she could give to herself. Something had to change!

The first thing that had to change was her mindset. For most women, especially mothers and especially military spouses, self-care is not even on their radar screens. With all the demands on your time, especially if you are dealing with a move or a deployment, time for yourself just doesn't happen. And it won't ever just happen. Like Holly, you have to change your thinking about the importance of taking care of yourself.

You are no real use to others if you are running on empty. Oh sure, you can manage it for a while. We all do. But keep running on empty and you'll end up crashing. If you are lucky, it will only be something like getting sick and having to stop for a short while. If you aren't lucky, it can be even more.

Holly's Story

I went to great lengths to work in exercise and time with my girlfriend, Cheryl Crosswaite. As moms of toddlers and preschoolers we would complain that our days were filled with work, maintenance, chores, and child-care duties. There never seemed to be time in the day to be able to talk as friends, let alone exercise. My three-year-old twins no longer wanted to sit in a stroller while I pushed them for exercise. Taking them out on their tricycles didn't work either. As any mother of twins will tell you, whenever you let go of twins' hands they immediately go in opposite directions—guaranteed. Cheryl was having similar problems with her children ages two and five.

We decided to take action. We took our four children to the local high school track, which had a big fence around the entire area. We put the children in the middle of the field with toys, balls, a wagon, a pop-up tent, and even a potty chair for those toilet-training moments. We told the children they were to play in the middle of the field while we exercised for thirty minutes. (For those of you who don't have children I am sure you are laughing at this point asking, "Why is this such a big deal?" Those of you who have (or had) toddlers and preschoolers know this is a big deal—asking toddlers to stay in one area while mommy walks away from them.)

But it did work—with a little effort and determination on our part. At first, Cheryl and I were only able to walk/run half way around and then back as to not be too far away from the children. We started out with fifteen minutes and increased our time with each successive day. Cheryl brought a timer and set it for thirty minutes so her five year old could understand when we would be finished exercising. There were times when the children would cry and want to run along side of us. We were consistent in telling them they could run with us, but we were not going to stop exercising until our thirty minutes was up. We helped each other be consistent and continued to increase our time. The children began to play more and more independently and even started cheering us on as we ran around the track.

I loved those times I had with Cheryl. We talked about our dreams, we brainstormed for each other, we held each other accountable, and we were friends helping the other person to become the best she could be. Everyone won in this scenario. Because Cheryl and I felt better about getting some time to talk with a friend and time to exercise our bodies, we felt better about our overall outlook on life. Our husbands even commented on the difference. We were happier and we had more energy for life—energy for our dreams, our children, our husbands, and ourselves.

You have to make the decision that self-care is important and a priority. After one of our workshops, we got an email from an Army spouse whose husband is deployed, leaving her with two young children. She said that we had given her the permission she somehow needed to hire a sitter once a week so she'd have some time to herself.

Hey, if you need permission, we hereby grant it to you.

Let's think about this—from whom are you waiting for permission? Your spouse? Your kids? Your community? As Dr. Phil McGraw says: "Obviously, a top priority is to be a good mother. But if you really care about your kids, you will take care of their mother." This is also true of fathers, but mothers somehow have a harder time with the concept. As Dr. Pamela Peeke, author of *Fight Fat Over 40 and Win* points out, "I tell my male patients they have to get out and exercise and they do it. I tell my female patients the same thing and they start talking about their children." She points out to these mothers that if they don't do some regular exercise to reach the ongoing calming effect exercise provides to them, they are choosing to be a cranky, stressed-out parent, ready to scream at the slightest provocation. Which kind of parent do you think your kids really want?

One woman we know finally got this concept as her two boys grew a bit older. "I used to love to take ballet class—before children," she says. "I'm no good at it, but it just plain energizes me and makes me grin from ear to ear." Recently, she started classes again. "I can't afford childcare," she adds. "So I told my boys, 'you can either sit on the sidelines quietly and draw or just sit and watch mommy, just like mommy always sits and watches you at swimming and soccer.'" She figures that it's important that they understand that mommy is a person too, with interests of her own.

Learn to Live Strategically

Remember, *knowing* what works and *doing* what works are two different things. We've both been there and still get to that same place sometimes—that place of knowing your daily actions are adding to your already high stress level but you are not making any changes. The starting point is to at least know what works and what doesn't when it comes to effectively managing your energy and stress levels.

You might want to think of this as living strategically. You don't have to give up all the things you enjoy—that might not be the best thing for you. What you can do instead is to give up things for certain periods of high stress when you know you need to be at your best. It's that 80/20 concept. If you make smart choices in activity and nutrition 80 percent of the time, that 20 percent of cake and coffee and chocolate won't hurt you in the long run.

We've asked lots of military spouses—especially those with the added time challenges of childcare—what works for them to keep their energy up and stress down. Here are the things we hear most often.

Learn to Say No

Learn how to build your "no" muscle. Not using this muscle seems to be the main obstacle keeping military spouses from putting themselves first. When you get clear that self-care is your priority, it is easier to say no to a request.

We are fully aware of the responsibilities that come with parenthood and know there are many requests that can't be ignored. We are also aware that there are many important community projects you may choose to take on, and friends and neighbors you'll choose to help out. But there are just as many times in your day when you are asked to do something you really don't want to do and to which you can say "no." You have a choice. Awareness is the first step. Pay attention to how often you do things you'd rather not do. Stop and pause before responding to a request. The key here is to learn to say no so you can say yes to the things you do want to do.

Let your family know at the beginning that you are going to make your self-care a priority and that you may say no to some of their requests. We have heard veteran spouse Susan speak at a conference. She described how she finally understood that she needed one evening a week for herself. So she held a family meeting to discuss this. As she said, "After all, what were they going to do, fire me?"

Don't you think it's time we start modeling to our children that each individual is important, including mom and dad? Saying no brings up the fear of disappointing or hurting others, of missing opportunities, and of making mistakes. But saying no means saying yes to *you*! No one else can do this but you. (You might want to take the Color Test described in chapter 10 on volunteering if you are living in overload because you aren't saying "no" enough.)

Know That You Have a Choice

You always have a choice to make changes. When your life seems out of control and you feel overwhelmed, you may think there is no way you can make changes right now. You feel like you don't have any choice but to continue doing what you've always been doing in order to survive

> *Learn to say no to things you can say no to, so you can say yes to the things you do want to do.*

day in and day out. This way of thinking leaves you with no energy and feeling joyless. Yet you do have the power to choose to make changes in your life.

For example, making choices about self-care might mean making some difficult choices like hiring someone to come in and watch the babies, trading off with another mother for some "me" time, or saying no to a request from someone else. That might mean being open about your needs and even—gulp—asking for help.

So many of us get caught up in limiting language such as: "have to" or "need to." We say, "I have to do the laundry." "I need to go to this meeting." Or, "I have to——(you fill in the blank.)" Those "have to" and "need to" words make us feel like powerless victims of circumstance. This is not where you want to be, and the choice truly is yours.

There is nothing you have to do if you are willing to pay the price for not doing it. Here's a simple example. If you choose not to do the laundry, then you are willing to pay the price for not doing it. By making the choice to do it, you are saying you "want to" or "choose to" do it. You would rather do it than not, even if it is something you don't really enjoy. Each one of us has a choice. Sometimes they are difficult choices, but nonetheless we do have a choice. Never confuse difficult choices with having no choices at all.

Just saying to yourself, "I choose to" or "I want to" instead of "have to" or "need to" gives the power back to you, the power to make the choices you want for your life. This self-power gives you energy that you need to move forward in your dreams. *You* have the power to make the choice.

Breathe

"I *stop* and *breathe*" is one of the most common things we hear from other moms when we ask them how they deal with stress.

The following magazine entry made us both laugh out loud: All mothers know how to do deep breathing if they went through Lamaze. "I remember my prenatal breathing. Those long deep breaths may have been useless during labor, but they sure do come in handy years down the road when you want to whack your kids but know you can't." —Lisa Wolfe, "Burying Zebra," in *Oprah* magazine.

Effective, conscious breathing is important for all of us. Most of us live on shallow chest breathing, holding our stomachs in and limiting our oxygen. We deprive ourselves of added energy from simple effective breathing. Take a deep breath, not just filling up your lungs, but actually taking a deep belly breath, and let the air out slowly. Say to yourself, "Stop and be present, take a deep breath, go slow." As you exhale, you might say the words, "Let Go and Relax." Do this right now. Close your eyes. See how you feel after stopping to take a deep breath.

We can all do that. It's an easy step that takes very little time. The hard part is to remember to do it. Holly wrote the word "Breathe" on 3 x 5 cards and put one in her car, one on her bathroom mirror, one on her kitchen windowsill, one on the telephone, and one above her computer. She found out quickly that her whining toddler was not going to suffer if mom stopped, stepped back, and took a deep breath. Everyone benefits when mom takes a moment to stop and *breathe*.

Kathie has the following two signs on her computer:

Breathing in, I calm body and mind
Breathing out, I smile
Dwelling in the present moment,
I know this is the only moment.
 —Thich Naht Hahn
Stop Doing! Just for this moment.
—SARK

You can use external triggers to remind you to breathe. Have you noticed how often you hold your breath as you go about your work? It's not uncommon to find yourself literally holding your breath as you concentrate on something you are doing. That raises your stress level and decreases your effectiveness in getting that job done.

When the telephone rings, purposely take a deep breath before you pick it up. For one thing, you'll be more present to the caller that way and it's a chance to remind yourself to breathe. Do the same thing with stoplights when you are driving the car. A red light means stop, take a deep breath (or two or three) and do shoulder shrugs to release tension.

For those times when you need a little extra stress reduction, stop to breathe and take a whiff of aromatherapy. The essential oil of lavender reduces our stress, while peppermint raises our energy. Find what works best for you.

You can use your breath and your thoughts in combination to help deal with extreme stress. Linda Beougher is an Army spouse who went through brain tumor surgery to remove a golf-ball sized tumor pressing against her brain stem. When we asked her how she managed her fears during that time, she shared a yoga breath exercise that helped her. It's an exercise we have both used many times since and have shared with spouses dealing with the current fears during Iraq deployments.

As you breathe in, say to yourself, "I breathe in trust, energy, lightness, faith" or whatever words speak to you. As you breathe out, say to yourself, "I breathe out fear, anxiety, fatigue," or whatever thoughts you want to be rid of. It seems simplistic, but this exercise can have a powerful effect on your day. Start and end your day with this exercise as a way to help keep fear and anxiety at bay. Linda reminds us, too, that this exercise is great for any time. Simply change the words and say, "I breathe in creativity, joy, abundance. I breathe out self-doubt, negativity, lack."

Dr. Martin Rossman is a physician, author, and educator known as a pioneer in the field of guided imagery, especially for cancer patients. As he points out, "When you worry about possible negative outcomes, that is imagery and it impacts negatively on how you feel." Using positive guided imagery, or a simple breath exercise can put you in a place of peace for a time, lowering your overall anxiety.

Take One Day at a Time

Many military spouses share this tool for how they manage this crazy lifestyle. When they plan their day, they schedule their self-care *first* and then work the rest of the demands and chores around their self-care time. That way it is never last on the list. Last things often get dropped, so put *you* first.

Stick to the motto: "Just for today, I can take care of myself. Just for today, I can make healthy choices when eating. Just for today, I can drink lots of water. Just for today, I can get to bed earlier. Just for today . . . ." Do not think about tomorrow or of losing ten pounds or of adding a full-fledged, long-term exercise program. What can you do today that will help you take care of yourself? Make that your priority for the day.

Think Movement, Not Exercise

Self-care is not about working out or losing weight. It is about taking care of you. When your life is packed with activity, the thought of adding a workout into that schedule sounds impossible. For one thing, the word itself sounds like work, like one more chore. Instead, say to yourself, "I want to add more movement into my day." You can do that for one day—just one day at a time. Just move!

We promise you: if you add some movement into your life, your energy will increase, your stress will decrease, and you will find yourself better able to handle the challenges thrown your way.

Here are some simple and fun ways to get more movement into your day:

- Get up from the computer, television, or from your chores and hula-hoop! Hey, it gets all the kinks out. One woman in our seminar told us her doctor advised her to hula-hoop to get her waist back after giving birth. It worked for her. It works for us to pump up our energy in a short amount of time. Army spouse Theresa Donahoe told us about the hula-hoops weighing three or five pounds designed specifically for waist trimming. Check out www.heavyhoop.com.

- Turn on your favorite music and dance around the house. You can do this by yourself or with your children. Get your kids dancing and picking up their toys at the same time—what fun!

- Park farther away from the store and walk to the entrance.

- Do something fun for you that has movement built in. From riding a bike to playing Frisbee with your dog to inline skating, fun movement beats "working out" every time.

- Keep toys in the trunk of your car. After picking up your children from school, stop at a park and play with them for a bit. You'll help them get some energy out, they will have fun with mom or dad, and you increase your energy for the rest of the day.

- One of the best things to do for your physical and emotional health is to walk and talk with a good friend. Think of it as "moving therapy."

- Use a pedometer and move. The pedometer keeps you honest about how much walking you really are getting in your day—and it's an incentive to increase that amount.

Sneak exercise into your day. Make it a game. Do squats while you blow-dry your hair or while you watch your kids practice soccer. Walk around the soccer field; you can still have your eyes on your child. Use the bench at the field for squats or reverse push-ups. Use the monkey bars for pull-ups. If you feel conspicuous doing that by yourself, enlist another parent to join you. You may start a trend.

For great ideas of things to do in short amounts of time, read *The Ultimate Guide of One-Minute Workouts for Anyone, Anywhere, Anytime,* by Bonnie Nygard, M.Ed., and Bonnie Hopper, M.Ed. It's a short book packed full of great ideas for simple things you can do at your desk, watching television, or doing your chores. Or check out the Fit Deck cards created by a Navy SEAL, with exercises you can do in one minute at www.fitdeck.com.

Dump Your Time and Energy Drains

If your life is so packed full that you think, "I can't add movement or weight training or meditation on top of all this," you are probably right. It is too full. Take something else off your list to make space. It's your health, longevity, and sanity we are talking about here.

Watching life on television does not beget energy. Participating in life does. Waiting for the perfect circumstances or some future date does not beget energy. Taking action does.

The kinds of things you might remove from your list include:

- Television watching. We aren't asking you to quit watching a great funny program that makes you laugh. We don't mean to cut out those shows that teach you new things, or movies that allow you a good laugh or cry. We suggest cutting out the kind of mindless TV watching that often happens, especially when you are tired, where you just sit as one show follows another, whether or not you are even interested, often finding it difficult to even go to bed and get the rest you so desperately need. More than any other activity, television watching promotes lethargy and passivity. You see it in your children. Well, it happens to adults too. You just don't feel like doing anything! The average American adult watches four to six hours of television each day. Cut out two or three of those hours and switch that time to healthy self-care and your dream project.
- Endless surfing of the Internet. Granted, there are great resources on the web. In fact, we share many in our resource list and wonder how we'd survive without email connection with our friends and Internet access for research. But maybe you are like us and have experienced the negatives attached to too much surfing. We have both at times ended up surfing the net late at night when we are already dead tired. "I'll just get on and check my email," we think. We surface hours later without any helpful new information, now totally exhausted with few hours left to sleep. Monitor

your use! One idea is to set a timer to go off at a specified time so that you stay aware of how long you are on.

One Army spouse said that she knew she couldn't handle a constant diet of television or Internet news while her husband was deployed, but she also didn't want to miss important news. She asked family members to do the surfing and let her know when they found an article about his unit.

- Reading the newspaper from cover to cover. This was Kathie's energy drain of choice for years. It's so accepted: "I need to keep up with the news." But imagine what a constant diet of negative news and images does to your energy. And that is what newspapers are full of. A better idea is to skim the headlines and read just what is important to you or truly interests you. Kathie likes to do this standing on her toes at the kitchen counter doing leg lifts. "Hey, if I sink into the couch my mind thinks I'm settling in for the duration," she says. "This way I keep it short *and* get some balance training and movement at the same time. Of course, when I can on the weekends I sometimes love to settle in for a read."
- Endless rambling telephone conversations. You need to connect with your friends and family. But you know when you've been on the phone too long, especially if you have fallen into gossiping and complaining about life. It's often a procrastination trap that keeps you from doing what you say you really want to do. If you need to talk, go outside and walk and talk with your friends. Turn an energy drain into an energy gain.
- Shopping out of boredom. This is especially problematic to those who truly are addicted to shopping, getting that high from buying. Your energy level and your checkbook don't need that. Try exercise or a creative pursuit instead. Or find art exhibits or museums to wander in rather than stores full of temptation.

Other common energy drains: clutter, procrastination, hanging out with negative people, unresolved conflicts, appliances that need repair, putting off important tasks like updating your will, and so on.

We all have our own energy drains. The key is to identify them and find ways to eliminate or limit them. It takes awareness and conscious choice. We recommend further reading on the issue of energy drains. Cheryl Richardson's book, *Take Time for Your Life,* has a great explanation in chapter 3. As she says, "What you may not know is that actions you don't take use energy—mental energy, emotional energy, energy that could be better used in a positive way." She includes a comprehensive checklist for you to identify your own energy drains.

Choose Foods and Beverages for Energy

We aren't about to tackle this extensive topic in full, but here are some basics. Think about eating and drinking strategically, based on what your choices do to your energy and stress levels. Eating small amounts of food, a mix of lean protein and complex carbohydrates every three to four hours will keep your energy up and your stress down. This is as simple as a whole-wheat cracker with almond butter or string cheese, or a handful (*just* a small handful) of raw almonds.

Watch your hydration.Water does matter since it makes up the largest percentage of our brain and our muscles. Dehydration is often the culprit when we are fatigued, and when we suffer from afternoon headaches and fuzzy thinking.

Dr. Monica Dixon is an Army spouse and mother who holds a doctorate in nutrition. She headed up a $1.2 million dollar grant program to make huge policy and initiative changes across Washington State in the areas of nutrition and physical activity. She's outspoken about small but important changes to make to improve your health and energy. Her number one bit of advice at a recent conference for women: "Quit drinking soda, yes, especially diet soda . . . and start drinking tea." Black, green, and white teas all have high levels of antioxidants, which help protect us against cancer and they aren't full of empty calories or chemicals."

We are happy to report something else that has high levels of antioxidants is dark chocolate. Of course, you have to limit yourself to small amounts because of the negative affects of sugar and fats and caffeine, but medical permission to eat chocolate is high on our list of Good News stories!

Turn Interests into Energy!

It's true. When you pursue your interests, you increase your energy level. Energy begets energy. Watching life on television does not beget energy. Participating in life does. Staying in your pajamas all day does not beget energy. Getting yourself dressed and out the door does. Waiting for the perfect circumstances or some future date does not beget energy. Taking action does.

This crazy military lifestyle is full of richness and possibilities, but your self-care needs to come first before you can even start to live life to its fullest. Take your first steps in saying *yes* to yourself—yes to self-care!— one step, one day at a time.

Resources

Breathing: The Master Key to Self-Healing, by Andrew Weil, MD (1999).
FitDeck card packs at www.fitdeck.com.
Guided Imagery for Self-Healing: An Essential Resource for Anyone Seeking Wellness, by Martin L. Rossman, MD (www.fightcancerwithin.com).

Heavy hoops at www.heavyhoop.com.

Softpower! How to Speak Up, Set Limits, and Say No Without Losing Your Lover, Your Job, or Your Friends, by Maria Arapakis (1990).

Strong Women Stay Young and Strong Women Stay Slim, and other books, by Miriam Nelson, MD (www.strongwomen.com).

Take Time for Your Life: A Personal Coach's Seven-Step Process for Creating the Life You Want, by Cheryl Richardson (1999).

The Ultimate Guide of One-Minute Workouts for Anyone, Anywhere, Anytime, by Bonnie Nygard, M.Ed., and Bonnie Hopper, M.Ed. (2000).

Time Management for Unmanageable People, by Ann McGee-Cooper with Duane Trammell (1993).

How to Say No Without Feeling Guilty and Say Yes to More Time, More Joy, and What Matters Most to You, by Patti Breitman and Connie Hatch (2000).

You Don't Have to Go Home Exhausted, by Ann McGee-Cooper [1992].

Chapter 7

Figure Out Who You Are
and What You Want

Exercises to Help You Figure Out Your Priorities, Strengths, and a Vision for Your Life

Know What You Want—And Why This Matters

So what do you want? What feeds your soul? Shouldn't that be easy to figure out? Shouldn't we naturally know what we want? Actually, it's not an easy thing for most of us. As Oprah says, "Have the courage to follow your passion—and if you don't know what it is, realize that one reason for your existence on earth is to find it . . . Your life's work is to find your life's work— and then to exercise the discipline, tenacity, and hard work it takes to pursue it." Do that and you'll live in what psychologist Mihaly Csikszentmihalyi calls "flow." Flow is the enjoyment you experience when you do something that stretches you beyond where you were before—in an athletic event, an artistic performance, a good deed, a stimulating conversation, a learning situation. Flow leads to personal growth and long-term happiness. Flow doesn't happen sitting passively watching television or complaining about your circumstances. Flow takes action on your part.

We used to think we each had only one mission in life and we needed to figure that one thing out. That's a bit scary. The more we talk to people and read and experience life, we think that passions change as life changes, as you get out and have new experiences and discover new things. It's just key that you find interests to get excited about during each stage of life.

As Randy Komisar, author of *The Monk and the Riddle,* says, "What I have come to understand is that we have a rich spectrum of passions. Why should we feel that one passion would guide us through our entire life? . . . A passion is constantly reenergizing you and bringing you to the next level of excitement and engagement in the world. It opens new doors, leads to new choices, and unlocks new passions in the process."

Here's one other way to think about this. Kathie attended a workshop with Cheryl Richardson, life coach and author of *Life Makeovers,* among other books. She told the audience that the number one question people ask her is "How do I find my purpose?" She said after years of working with people she believes there are really two reasons for our lives. The first is to make our own personal development, our own spiritual development a priority "to become the best spirit you can be." The second purpose is to contribute to others in some meaningful way. So the question is more about "How can I live my life to spend time on those two key purposes?"

Develop Whole-istic Dreams

Before we discuss your dreams and your purpose in life, we want to address two key concepts.

1. When we talk about "following your dreams," we have an image of a very holistic dream. Maybe we should call it a "whole-istic" dream. In other words, when figuring out what your dreams in life are, it's important to consider all aspects of your life. You want to be sure to ask yourself the question: "How do I want my life as a whole to be?"

As Gregg Levoy, author of *Callings,* says, "Dreams are more interested in the design and quality of our lives than in making us rich and famous."

Why have a whole-istic approach? We've seen too many people (ourselves both included at times) who focus on one dream. That might be a career dream, an education dream, maybe even a parenting dream. If you focus too narrowly on one area of your life—if you spend all of your time, energy, and attention on that one area to the total exclusion of others—you might achieve that one dream, but at what cost?

We all know individuals who have done that or who are in the process of doing that.

- The military member who devotes every living minute and all his attention to his military career, constantly shorting his family, friends, and himself. Mind you, there are times they have no choice but to do that, like during war and deployments and certain high-stress positions. We're talking of the ones who never manage to turn off that ramped-up crisis-management mode even when they are in a peacetime assignment or on vacation. Many carry that same nonstop 24/7 work pattern into the civilian workforce after military life. Unfortunately, our military culture does a lot to promote that thinking. It takes a conscious choice to fight that trend.

- The military spouse who gets so caught up in the volunteer position she is passionate about that she neglects her family, her spouse and herself—and sometimes even her health. Volunteering is a wonderful thing and the military community benefits greatly from our many volunteers. But there can be too much of a good thing when it negatively affects your family and your health.
- The parent who can't make any time for her spouse, her friends, or herself. Certainly you make many sacrifices in life for your children. But focusing all your time, energy, and attention solely on your children isn't good for you—or for them.

If you are like Kathie, a "recovering" workaholic and perfectionist, you might recognize this syndrome in yourself. At different times in Kathie's life, she managed to focus solely on one area—in her case her career. At times that career wasn't even her dream. When she did start working on her dream business, her single-minded, workaholic tendencies crept right back in. There's a big danger in this. Unless your dream project is something that can fully sustain you in all areas forever, you are cutting off important aspects of life.

Another reason the wholistic approach is so important is this. Say your career is everything to you. Then the military moves you to a place where you really can't pursue that particular career. If all you have is your career—if your whole ego is dependent on that position—you are going to be miserable for that assignment. But if you have holistic dreams, you can see that location as an opportunity to put your time and energy into another interest, another facet of your life.

In fact, research shows that if one area of your life is not working well and is difficult for you to change, you can improve your overall quality of life—your happiness—by making improvements in the other areas of your life.

In a whole-istic life dream, here are some areas to consider: health and physical fitness, self-esteem, finances, work, play, learning, creativity, helping, love, friends, children, relatives, home, spiritual life, neighborhood, and community.

2. Start out fully aware of your current abundance. Identify and be grateful for what you already have in your life. We know people who are so focused on future dreams and goals that they never stop to appreciate the joys staring them in the face. If you focus only on what's missing, your life becomes negative and narrow. You fall into poverty thinking—that "glass is half empty" thinking. Poverty thinking will not help you move toward any dream. So start out with that gratitude journal. You'll quickly find yourself wallowing in abundance. That's a much better place to start from when you go for your dreams.

What do you want to take action on? What's important to you? Get your journal ready for some exercises. It can be truly amazing to look back on these exercises later in life to see how much of what you dreamed about comes true.

And remember, we can't emphasize this enough: the research on happiness shows us our overall satisfaction in life comes from identifying what we want and working toward it in some manner. Reaching your vision is not the definitive answer to overall happiness in life. It's the fact that you have figured out what it is you want and you are taking action, taking steps (and sometimes they are baby steps) no matter where you are located or what your circumstances are at the time.

Start with the Ideal Life Exercise

A great starting point to figure out what you want, what your passions are, where your purpose lies, is the Ideal Life exercise.

Kathie's Story

I first did this exercise when I took a personal growth seminar offered by the Women's Resource Center at the University of Richmond when Greg was stationed at Fort Lee, Virginia. Since I'm a pack rat, I still have that description: "I get up in the morning when my body feels like getting up without an alarm clock going off. I walk out onto the deck overlooking the water with my mug of rich coffee in hand. I enjoy a breakfast of fruit and granola while I read a newspaper or a book, easing into my day. Then I start into my workday, reading, writing, talking with people on the phone." At the time we lived in the city and I started my day early, packing my car to get out on the road in my job as a pharmaceutical sales rep. My breakfast was usually a quick bacon biscuit and weak coffee at Roy Rogers while I planned my calls. A far cry from my ideal.

A number of years later, I was talking on the telephone to an interesting woman as I looked out at our deck overlooking the water. It hit me that I was living close to my ideal day. (I'd gotten up earlier and had my breakfast of fruit and Grapenuts and good coffee sitting out on the deck.) Okay, I only get to spend occasional weeks or days at the coast. We aren't quite there fulltime yet, but I'm definitely moving closer to that dream.

Since that day of awareness, my life has developed even closer *to my dream of becoming a full time writer, as I write regular columns, articles, and this book, with many more books planned. Did it happen by magic? No. I think clarifying the dream is the first important step towards making it a reality.*

The key to doing this exercise is to take a little reflection time, time off by yourself with no distractions. Send everyone off to the movies or get a sitter or trade childcare with a neighbor. Go off to a café or the library (someplace where your phone won't ring and your laundry piles won't scream at you.) Open yourself to possibilities. Don't limit yourself in any way. This Ideal Life exercise is an exercise in dreaming, and DREAM BIG! Pretend we are waving a magic wand and granting you whatever you want. If you had a perfect life, an ideal life, what would it look like? Write your description in first person and present tense as if it is already your world. Include as much detail as possible.

- What would you be doing, both for work and for play?
- What kinds of people would you be involved with on a regular basis? Maybe they are artistic people, or children, or computer wizards, or dramatic people. What kinds of people energize you?
- What kinds of relationships would you have? How would ideal relationships be with your spouse, children, extended family, coworkers, or neighbors?
- What would your family life look like on a daily basis?
- What kind of spiritual practice would you have?
- What personal characteristics do you have? Describe who you are. Would you be powerful or self-confident or playful or childlike or dramatic or outrageous? Consider the characteristics you admire in others.
- How about your appearance? For example, what kinds of clothes would you wear,and how would you wear your hair?
- Where are you living this perfect life? What's your environment? Is it a specific place in the world or a more general description of a place? Include your immediate environment—your bedroom, house, office, yard, or balcony.
- What pace would you like for your life on a daily basis?
- What might you be doing to give back to the greater community?

No two people's ideal life descriptions will be the same. Kathie's description runs three typed pages and it keeps changing as she discovers new things and changes her mind (you're allowed to change your mind). Her husband's is two-thirds of a page. Holly's is ten hand-written pages. Holly's Army engineer husband has his on index cards in bullet format! The format doesn't matter. Just get it in writing.

By the way, it's a really good idea to ask your spouse to do this exercise too. You want to work toward mutual goals and dreams as a couple and as a family. The first step is identifying them, and, in the case of couples, look at areas you might need to work out some win/win compromises. The research on successful marriages conducted by Dr. John Gottman indicates that working toward mutual goals and dreams is key to a good relationship.

Once you do your ideal life description, it's a great idea to ask a group of friends for theirs too. Read them out loud to each other. This does a couple of things. You will be amazed at what other people come up with as they truly dream *big*. You may find that although you try not to limit yourself at all, you may very well do so in your first attempt at writing your ideal life. Often your initial description is not your ideal life. It is your much smaller idea of what is possible for you, limited especially by moving with the military. Hearing the others stretch will give you the courage to dream *big* for yourself. Reading your description aloud also starts a magical process. Things

Once others know your dreams, they'll help you in ways you would never have imagined possible.

start to happen. Resources and people show up in your life. Synchronicity and serendipity step in to help. Once others know your dreams, they'll help you in ways you would never have imagined possible.

So what do you do with your description?

Step One. Highlight everything in your description that is already in your life and first give gratitude for them. Second, take steps to make sure you keep them. Because sometimes when we take wonderful things for granted, they go away. Whether it's our health or our good relationships, if we do nothing to sustain these, they can disappear. Write down an action plan of what you will do to keep these fresh and vital.

Step Two. Figure out, what's in your description that you can add into your current physical environment? We guarantee that there are ways you can do that, no matter where you are stationed, no matter how dismal your current quarters might be.

For example, Kathie's ideal environment includes living on the water with a beautiful "secret" garden near the mountains with green all around. It also includes wall-to-wall, floor-to-ceiling, built-in bookshelves, a wood-burning stove, a big overstuffed chair and ottoman, and a cat in her lap.

When she wrote her ideal description, she and Greg lived on the top floor of an old building in downtown Richmond, Virginia, not near the water or mountains. There were no bookshelves, no wood-burning stove, no garden, no yard at all. She did have two cats. (And she was grateful for them and took good care of them; they lived to be twenty and twenty-one!) Since that time, she's lived in Washington state, Kansas, Germany, Oregon, and now back in Washington state. Until recently, she didn't live near the water. Until Oregon she did not have a garden. But in all those places she carried her ideal environment with her—big photos of the ocean and the mountains in her home office, a crystal box filled with sand and shells to remind her of the ocean. Cards with beautiful flowers on her desk and fresh flowers whenever she can afford them. All of those things bring her daily joy; they change her daily experience of life. We don't know if it's the memory of things or the anticipation of things or just the beauty of these things. But they can bring joy, especially if you are stuck in some of those quarters that were built as temporary dwellings in World War II!

Put more emphasis on changing what you can to make your environment work for you and your family as you move with the military. This exercise is a good start. Awaken your five senses to make your home warm and inviting. When your senses are stimulated in a positive way, any experience becomes more enjoyable. (For more ideas on how to enhance your current environment check out a free report on our website at militaryspousehelp.com.)

Step Three. The third thing that will come out of this description is some of your bigger goals in life. Goal setting is one of the most important skills to master as you move toward your dreams. We'll spend a whole chapter on goal-achieving techniques.

Get Input from Your Friends and Family

We read a great idea in the book *Inc. Your Dream* by Rebecca Maddox. Ask a dozen friends and family members the following questions and see what trends come out.

- If you didn't know what I did for a living, what would you see me doing?
- Describe me to a friend in one to two words.
- What would you like to see me develop in myself?
- What do you see as my driving force or passion?
- If I didn't have to make a living at it, what would you see me doing?

The answers to those questions might remind you of things you'd forgotten or taken for granted. Sometimes the obvious is staring us in the face, but we are too close to it to see.

Forget the "Shoulds" and Comparisons

As you create your vision of your ideal life, there are some things best left out: "shoulds" and comparisons.

When Kathie first wrote a column for the *Army Times* in 1997, one reader's letter stopped her short: "A year and a half ago, when I wanted to take a job, my husband casually mentioned it at work. His buddies said he shouldn't let me because he works and goes to the field and busts his butt all day long, and why shouldn't he come home to a clean house and dinner on the table? It didn't stop there. For the next two weeks practically every wife I knew was calling or stopping by to tell me how unfair it would be to my husband and children."

Kathie was reminded of an assertiveness training workshop she once took with a mix of military spouses and civilian employees in Germany. As they went around the room explaining why they were each there, one comment struck Kathie. An Army spouse said that she was choosing to stay home with her kids rather than continue the career she had before marrying into the military. "I know it is the right choice for me. I just want to become more assertive in answering the question, 'What do you do?' and in dealing with the perception that I'm a lesser person because I choose not to work outside the home right now."

The point isn't whether or not we should work or go to school or stay home with our kids. It isn't whether we should volunteer in our military community or get involved with our church or civilian community. It isn't whether we should decorate our front door with each new season or create the perfect lawn. The point is that whatever we choose to do should be our own choice based on our needs and interests and situations. Our choice also should be made based on discussions within our own family, not on "shoulds" we hear from other military spouses, from our military culture, or from society at large.

Here's the reality. We get a lot of "shoulds" thrown at us in life. First our parents have ideas of who we should be and how we should dress and how we should act. Then our peers head us in different directions. Then our spouse has ideas for us. Even our kids have ideas of how we should dress and act, especially our teenagers. On top of all that we have society's expectations—or at least how we interpret society's expectations. Finally, add the military community's expectations. Although things are changing in this military world, there are still a lot of spoken and unspoken expectations of military spouses.

As Babette Maxwell, cofounder of *Military Spouse* magazine says, "Often in military life, who you are as a person seems not to count. I've often thought I should get my husband to give me a Power of Attorney for the right to be me! You know, 'I hereby allow my wife to be who she is, to sign as herself.' Maybe with that I could claim my own identify. It would be validation that I count."

Here's the problem. When we have layers of shoulds thrust on us, it's often tough to sift through and answer the questions, "What are my priorities? What do I value? How do I want to live my life? Who is the real me?" Sometimes we think we want something and then realize that we really don't want it at all. We just thought we did because everyone else said we "should" want it. So, it's not an easy thing to do, ignoring the shoulds, but it's crucial.

If we as military spouses don't push to be seen and treated as individuals, to be given power in our own right instead of as appendages or dependents, things won't change. We've seen some incredible changes in the status of military spouses over the twenty-plus years we've been connected to the military. And they came about because enough spouses spoke up. There is still a lot of room for improvement. We hope to continue to see positive changes. The place to start is in claiming our own authenticity.

Holly's Story

I arrived in Germany pregnant with twins, my first pregnancy. No sooner did I come home from the hospital with our twins than my husband's unit deployed for a ten-month mine-clearing mission in Bosnia. Yes, we all know deployments are a possibility but when they happen, we think "Why now—why us?" We had tried for twelve years to get pregnant. Finally we have twins and my husband is leaving?! To top it off, one of the twins, Jack, was the classic nightmare baby, never sleeping more than forty-five to fifty minutes at a time, and screaming all the time. The poor darling had horrible reflux and I literally wore a raincoat every time I fed him, because half of what I fed him landed all over me. The only way I could comfort him (and me) was to wear him in a sling for the first nine months. My other baby, Helen, was considered by my friends as a "high needs" baby. If Helen was a high needs baby, Jack was an "insatiable needs" baby. I would go days without sleep. I felt so alone, even though I had other wonderful military spouses around me willing to help. (It took me time to learn to accept help.)

How could I feel so alone with so much support around me? I didn't look at it as support—I saw all these other mothers whose husbands were deployed handling life much better than I was. I felt I should be able to handle things better than I was. I felt I should be able to take my new parenting role in stride like so many others seem to. I felt I should be able to help other spouses from the unit deal with the deployment challenges. I felt I should be able to keep my house clean and keep myself looking presentable. I felt I should get regular letters and care packages off to my husband like so many other spouses were doing. I was should-ing all over myself—no wonder I felt so down.

If you find yourself doing what Holly did, stop right now! Say these words out loud. "I am doing the best I can right now under the circumstances I am in and I am proud of myself. I don't have to be the best mom in the world; I just have to be the best mom I can be." What you want to do is stop the negative thoughts that are beating you up as soon as possible. There is enough negativity in the world to beat us up. You certainly do not need to be your own worst enemy. During times of stress you need as many allies surrounding you as possible—no better place to start than with yourself. Our *should*-ing problem doesn't take place only during deployments. We need to be aware of our self-talk every day.

"One of the most important questions you can ask yourself: Have I defined what success means to me or am I working my butt off based on someone else's definition?" —Oprah

Adopt the "As Is" Philosophy

There's a related challenge that we all face. Many of us waste a lot of time and energy comparing ourselves to other people and coming up short in our own estimation.

Kathie's Story

For years I compared myself to other people and especially to this person I now realize was a myth, the "good military wife." I had this idea that to be a good military wife myself I had to be this person. I had to be outgoing and naturally talkative. I had to be well organized. I wanted to be one of those people who could just move a household, settle in , and get new curtains up in two weeks even though the windows are all a different size than the previous place. (I don't sew at all so that's a big order.) I wanted to be one of those people who always cook a great potluck dish—the kind that is eaten early and everyone asks for the recipe. (I always end up taking my dish back home for the next few night's meals.) I wanted to be one of those people who always knows the right thing to say and the right thing to do, especially in emergency situations. But I wasn't that person.

For years I beat myself up about it. I can't sew, I can't cook, and I am not naturally organized. I'm naturally an introvert, and I don't react well in emergency situations. I finally understood after many years that I have strengths too. They may be different strengths but they're strengths. It's okay that I don't have those other strengths. Our military family and society at large is really much better off because we do all have different strengths. If we all had the exact same strengths, it would be a pretty boring and probably extremely dysfunctional world!

We have noticed that most of us do not simply compare ourselves to one other individual. Oh no, that might actually be realistic. No, we tend to do things just a little bit bigger than that. Here's what many of us do.

We look at one person and think, "She has her career all figured out. She knows what she wants and she is taking steps and moving forward. *I can't even find a job and I feel a little bit stuck.*" And then we beat ourselves up. Then we look at another person and think, "She is such a great parent. She does all these fun, artistic, creative things with her kids. *I have a hard time just doing the basics.*" And then we beat ourselves up. Then we look at someone else and think, "She is in such great shape. She runs regularly and works out with weights three times a week. *I hardly do any exercise at all.*" And then we beat ourselves up. Then you look at someone totally different and think, "Her house is so organized and spotless. She can even get her car in the garage. *I don't even make my bed unless I know company is coming and our car will never see the inside of our garage.*" And then we beat ourselves up.

That is not one other person; those are four or five or more other people we are idealizing for comparison. We are comparing ourselves to a myth—to a super person—a creature that doesn't even exist. Of course we come up short! Then we wonder why we feel like failures. We wonder why we feel overloaded with all the things we feel we still have to do.

Here's the reality. Military spouses are incredible! But when we spend time comparing ourselves to others and trying to live up to everyone else's expectations—we often lose ourselves in the process. We lose our power and our true sense of self. We end up trying to pretend to be someone we aren't. That's an impossible pretense to keep up over the long haul. A great passage in Rita Mae Brown's novel *Venus Envy* reads, "The trouble with conforming is that everyone likes you except you." It's time we stop doing that. Let's adopt a different philosophy. The philosophy of "As Is."

Our favorite piece of jewelry is a pewter pin that says "As Is." Kathie's been wearing one for many years. Here's the interesting thing. Most people will come up to her when they see that and say, "As is—I love that—great concept." Others will come up and look confused. Then they sometimes ask hesitantly, "So who's ASIS (rhyming with basis)?"

Kathie readily admits she isn't quick on her feet. The first few times that happened, she went through a long convoluted explanation of what "As Is" means. But now she has the answer. Now whenever anyone says, "Who's ASIS?" she immediately replies, "Oh, ASIS is the Egyptian goddess of reality and I'm one of her disciples. I believe in her philosophy and I'm spreading that philosophy."

The artist who created that pin is Lena Guyot. She includes a card with each pin that explains her own concept of As Is.

"As Is—On the journey of the self, there comes a time when we make peace with who we are, respecting our strengths and accepting our weaknesses. We cease to sit in judgment on ourselves or others and get on with life. 'As Is' is a proud declaration to the world and a reminder to ourselves that we are already quite wonderful, just the way we are."
©1994, LENA GUYOT, WITH PERMISSION

Here's our interpretation:

"As Is. Flaws and all." Take me or leave me—as is. Accept me despite my weaknesses. I'm great just as I am. I might be working toward my goals to make changes in things I'm not thrilled about. There is the conscious choice factor there. But I don't beat myself up over those things. I accept them lovingly as I work to make changes. Some of my weaknesses I just plain accept and stop trying to change. I realize they aren't weaknesses at all—they are just areas that aren't my particular strong suits.

Our greatest happiness comes from using our strengths in life, applying those strengths for the greater good. That's a much better idea than focusing on our weaknesses.

"Be yourself. It's a tough act to follow."—Katharine Hepburn

Celebrate Your Strengths

We often focus on the lack in ourselves—the things we need to improve or fix. Very often we don't stop to recognize or even acknowledge what is already a strength.

A passage from *Meditations for Women Who Do Too Much,* by Anne Wilson Schaef, reads: "It is much easier to see what we haven't done rather than to see what we have done. Often, if we just stop and take stock, we really have accomplished quite a bit. In fact, we probably are a wee bit close to the edge of working wonders. Unfortunately, we miss the opportunity to marvel at our wonders because we have so much set up still to do that what we have done pales into insignificance in relation to what is always yet to be done."

As military spouses, we are even more guilty of this. If we really thought about it, we often are "working wonders," especially during times of deployments, moves, and other challenges of military life. But we don't often give ourselves credit (partially because we can always point out someone who seems to have it harder than we do or seems to have it more together than we do).

What we really need is an "I love me" wall like our spouses have. Only instead of having graduation certificates or unit awards, it would show things such as:

- Packed up and moved the house by myself,
- Survived a deployment even with a car and toilet breaking down,
- Reestablished the kids and self once again in a new place with no immediate support.

Give yourself credit and a pat on the back for these accomplishments.

When we've mentioned this in our workshops, we've had some spouses roll their eyes and say, "Well, of course, we've all had to do those things." That attitude negates the fact that those are accomplishments, a show of great strength, whether every other military spouse has managed to do the same or not. Our civilian friends are in awe of these accomplishments. Their comments: "Move nineteen times in twenty-five years? Oh, I could never do that! I struggled with just two moves so far in my lifetime! Deal with your husband being gone for a year in a dangerous place? I can hardly cope when he's gone for a week-long business trip."

Military spouses are awesome. Give yourself credit!

We find it ironic that military spouses used to be called dependents, when most of them are the most independent people we've ever met.

Holly's Story

I don't want to say military spouses are better than other spouses, but I do believe there is a difference. Every military spouse I know has handled some major emergency on their own during deployments or TDYs, from car problems to plumbing problems to whatever. Military spouses just plain learn to handle things.

One of my favorite stories is of Sarah Selvidge, an Army spouse.

While she was living overseas and her husband was deployed for ten months, her car engine gave out. She found a mechanic who was willing to fix her car if she could get another engine. Amazingly, the next thing I knew she was on her way to the junkyard to "pluck an engine" out of another car. It was something she had never done before in her life, but knew she had to do in order to have transportation. Not only did she "pluck" that engine, but she even assisted the mechanic in getting the car running again. "I am woman— hear me roar!"

Identify Your Strengths So You Can Celebrate Them

We are often too close to this to do it for ourselves. Here's one idea. Photocopy the following list of positive characteristics. Give a copy to family members and friends and ask them to check off the strengths they see in you and to star your top ten strengths. Before you look at what they mark, do the same for yourself.

Your friends will likely identify strengths you simply take for granted, that you don't even recognize as strengths. So read them carefully and pat yourself on the back for having developed and nourished those strengths!

There is another aspect to this exercise. If you check off characteristics on your sheet and no one else checks that same characteristic, it might be one of those blind spots we sometimes have about ourselves. It might actually be a weakness we aren't aware of. For example, if you check off "good listener" and not one other person who knows you well checks that box, you might want to step back and pay attention to your listening skills and habits. And of course, choose to work on that area only if you care to.

Choose Your Battles—Or Choose Your Weakness

- Make a list of three weaknesses you know you have that you choose to address. Make sure it's a priority of your own to strengthen these particular weaknesses. Then come up with one to two action steps you can take for each one. Discuss this with a friend for added accountability.
- Make a list of three weaknesses that you are willing to "let go." They don't matter enough to you to spend your time and energy on, considering the other things in life that you do want to spend your time on. Write these on a slip of paper and burn it. Don't waste another minute worrying about those weaknesses! You might want to share this with your friend too so they can remind you if you forget to let go and end up obsessing about them again.

My Strengths

Please look through this list and circle any characteristics you think
I have. Then star what you see as my top ten strengths.

friendly	funny	smart	organized
focused	confident	assertive	helpful
patient	outrageous	dramatic	artistic
caring	good listener	detail-oriented	disciplined
logical	proactive	balanced	decisive
mediator	creative	nurturing	enthusiastic
positive	optimistic	cooperative	objective
responsible	playful	leader	calm
problem-solver	studious	kind	honest
cheerful	persistent	energetic	risk-taker
steady	passionate	joyful	insightful
take charge	forgiving	aware	persuasive
professional	elegant	gracious	gentle
connector	powerful	modest	fun
present	peaceful	sharing	courageous
good parent	involved	independent	eccentric

Others:

_____ _____ _____ _____

_____ _____ _____ _____

_____ _____ _____ _____

Create Your Life List:
101 Things I Want to Do, Be, Have in My Life

Lou Holtz, the famous football coach, was twenty-eight years old, had just lost his job, had no money in the bank, and his wife Beth was pregnant with their third child. He was so discouraged that Beth gave him the book *The Magic of Thinking Big*, by David J. Schwartz to lift his spirits. The book suggested you write down all the goals you want to achieve before you die.

Holtz sat down and wrote down one hundred and seven impossible goals. His list included things like having dinner at the White House, being coach of the year, making a hole in one, jumping out of an airplane.

We've heard this described as making the future enticing enough to pull you toward it, to take steps, to take action. Of the one hundred and seven goals Holtz wrote down in 1966, he has achieved eighty-one. That's the power of identifying what you want!

Kathie's Story

I first tried to write down 101 things I wanted in life in 1992. "Learn Italian, have a successful TV show, publish successful books, learn ballroom dancing, learn to garden, kayak in Alaska, hike in Utah . . ." I ran out of ideas at about forty. I figured I could keep adding places I want to hike, kayak, and cross country ski at, but even with that I ran out of wishes at sixty-four.

When I mentioned this to my success group in Heidelberg, Germany, Gail Howerton said, "Oh, I have one of those lists. I sat on a mountain side and made mine up after attending a seminar back in 1980." She found it and showed it to us. We were all amazed at how many things on her list she had already achieved.

Seeing her list gave me a big "Ah, hah." I hadn't included many "to be" items. So I started adding them: be more self-confident and trust my instincts, be more spontaneous, become comfortable with technology. I also started adding people I want to meet: SARK, Natalie Goldberg, Madeleine L'Engle. So I got to 101.

So, why have this list? Won't it be discouraging if you don't get it all? We don't think so. It's a good exercise to stretch yourself to think of all the wonderful possibilities in this world. It is another way to start to identify goals. It opens you up to all kinds of opportunities.

But be careful what you wish for; you may get it. As Norma Jean Saunders, the first woman to climb Mount McKinley solo, said in an interview, "There are certain things I would like to do, certain climbs I would like to make. They're not ambitions, exactly, just daydreams. But that can be kind of scary. I have to be careful what I dream about, because everything I've dreamed has come true."

Kathie admits that she isn't the most organized person in the world, especially when it comes to files. She lost her 101 list for many years. When she found it as we started writing the book, we were impressed with how many things have already come true. She had only tried kayaking once through the Fort Lewis Recreation Center when she first wrote the list. Since then she and her husband have indeed "kayaked in Alaska, kayaked in Baja, kayaked in the San Juan Islands," all items on that list. She had only just started writing (after years of saying "someday I want to be a writer"), but she wrote down "write a column for the *Army Times*." Now where did that come from—talk about dreaming way outside the realm of the possible? Who knows where that came from, but she ended up writing a column for the *Army Times* for a year in 1997, and since 2003 we've cowritten a column for the *Air Force, Army, Navy,* and *Marine Corps Times* newspapers.

She had included "trek to Nepal" to that list after reading a book by Jennifer James about her trek. Kathie admits she considered that particular item a "someday" thing probably meant for retirement years. She certainly wasn't doing any actual goal-setting things to make it happen. Then in 1993, the opportunity to go to Nepal fell into her lap. Her new friend and support group member, Gail, had been planning a Nepal trip for more than a year, doing all the research, talking to people who had done it, corresponding with people in Nepal. She had planned the trip for herself and some friends who suddenly backed out. Kathie and Greg got to take their place without a bit of work on their part.

So make up your list of 101. Who knows where it might lead!

Some Good Questions to Ask Yourself as You Write Your List:
- Who are your role models? What is it about their lives that appeals to you?
- If you could apprentice with anyone, who would that be?
- Where would you like to go?
- What would you like to see?
- What would you like to share?

Start Your Heart's Desires File

If you don't currently have time to do any of these exercises, you can start in a quick simple way for now. Get a basket or file folder. For the next few months as you read magazines or newspapers, cut out (or for now simply tear out) photos or articles or headlines that appeal to you. Include any visuals that you love—they might be postcards or advertising mailers or photos from catalogs or travel magazines. They might be articles about what other people have done. Don't think about it too much—just tear them out and put them in your basket or file.

After a few months, sit down with a cup of tea and your favorite music playing and browse through your file. See if there are any patterns, any themes. This can give you a good idea of what you want in your life, of the goals you might want to work toward, or of the kinds of work and activities or community projects you might want to get involved with—of the kind of person you'd like to be.

> *Helping/serving others in need is a powerful way to connect to your passion and to increase your joy in life.*

As Oprah says, "Pay attention to what makes you feel energized, connected, stimulated—what gives you your juice."

Hang on to the file. It will come in handy when you read the goals chapter. You'll have a head start on your Treasure Map.

Identify a Passion to Help Others

Look back on your life. Have you overcome a major challenge? You can often use this experience and the wisdom you've gained from it to help others who face the same challenge. Helping/serving others in need is a powerful way to connect to your passion and to increase your joy in life. Don't forget, the feeling that you are making a difference in someone else's life is one of the top routes to joy and may just be one of the central purposes for all of us in life.

In the next chapters, we'll look at three possible areas of interest for military spouses—career, business, or volunteering. Then, no matter which area interests you (and mind you, this can apply to hobbies as well), we'll spend time on how to move toward what you want and how to get the support you need to do so.

Action Steps

Pick one of the exercises to do this week. Share with a friend. Writing things down and speaking the words out loud starts a process. Schedule the other exercises over the next month or so. Write them into your calendar.

Resources

Callings, by Gregg Levoy [1998].

How to Think Like Leonardo da Vinci: Seven Steps to Genius Every Day, by Michael Gelb (1998). Although this is about creativity, there is a lot about life and passion exploration in here.

Inc. Your Dream, by Rebecca Maddox [1996].

Living Life on Purpose: A Guide to Creating a Life of Success and Significance, by Greg Anderson (1997).

Meditations for Women Who Do Too Much, by Anne Wilson Schaef [1996, rev. 2004].

The Artist's Way: A Spiritual Path to Higher Creativity, by Julian Cameron (1992) Great life exploration exercises whether you are an artist or not.

The Path: Creating a Mission Statement for Work and for Life, by Laurie Beth Jones (1996).

The Monk and the Riddle, by Randy Komisar [2001].

The Magic of Thinking Big, by David J. Schwartz [1987].

Venus Envy, by Rita Mae Brown (1994).

Wishcraft, by Barbara Sher, and her other books, *Living the Life You Love, I Could Do Anything if I Only Knew What It Was, It's Only Too Late if You Don't Start Now.*

Women and the Blues: Passions That Hurt, Passions That Heal, by Jennifer James (1988).

Chapter 8

How Can I Pursue a Career
While I'm Married to the Military?

Finding Meaningful Work as You Move

Be Aware of the Realities

The simple answer? It isn't easy! Sure there are some career fields that lend themselves more readily to this mobile lifestyle than others. But even in those fields, there are sometimes challenges with moving state to state and out of the country. Just the move itself and the time involved finding, starting, and learning a new position affect your career path.

So . . . is it even possible? Well, we aren't going to tell you that you can pursue a straight-line path in your career, something you might manage to do if you stayed in one place. Yes, there are exceptions. Two that come to mind are Marty and Karen, both Army wives. They managed to move their career specialist roles with an Army contractor with each move, continuing without break. When they moved to the Washington, DC, area, they were able to step into positions at the parent company headquarters. In their cases, they did manage to progressively move up, not facing job searches or breaks in service with each move. This points out that contacting companies that have long-standing contracts with the military is one option to consider as you conduct a job search. With many more military services contracted out these days, it's certainly worthy of consideration. It's also a place where your military tie is an immediate plus.

Another example is Coast Guard spouse Elaine Wilhelm-Hass. Elaine is in nursing and nursing administration, career fields with jobs more readily available just about anyplace. And with our aging population, the need for nurses keeps growing. During her twenty-five years of being married to the military,

Elaine has moved more than fifteen times and has been able to find a job with each move, each one generally paying better than the one before.

Cydnee Gentry is a Marine Corps spouse who has moved ten times in fifteen years. She has been able to find jobs in her field of education with each move. "Education is a great field and I've never had a problem finding a teaching job or a job working with kids."

Navy spouse Doreen Griffith, a certified public accountant (CPA) with a bachelor's degree in accounting and a specialty in taxation, has managed to work as a tax professional doing tax planning and compliance for corporations and high net worth individuals throughout sixteen years and seven moves with the military. Even changing companies with each move, she was recently promoted to partner for Grant Thornton, the fifth largest accounting firm in the United States.

Check out the resource section of this chapter for articles on mobile career fields like education, healthcare, finance, and many others.

But what if your chosen career field isn't easily mobile? Plus, even the "mobile career fields" have challenges because of this life. Here are the basic difficult realities of this mobile life for most of us:

- You lose time with each move to the logistics of the move and unpacking itself, and to the time spent in a job search. Average job searches take from four to nine months—and that's from when you start the search. If you wait until you are moved and have the family settled in, as many of us do, you add to that time.
- You sometimes have to start at lower income levels with each move, having to prove yourself all over again with a new employer.
- You may not find available work that fits your career field in some places, especially in overseas assignments.
- You may not be able to take promotions or other opportunities with a company you work for if they mean moving yourself to do so (unless you choose to have a distance marriage for a time as some military couples have done).
- You may find it difficult to give your job your all when you are acting as a single parent during a long deployment, responsible for all house and childcare activities during a time when children need even more of your energy and attention than usual. (We know spouses who have chosen to quit work during those times. Even though they know it was the right decision for them, that decision adds additional holes to their resumes.)
- You might have to spend time and money to recertify in each new state as you move, depending on the requirements for your career field.

- You most likely will not be able to continue in a career or company long enough to provide you with any kind of retirement pension.

Trying to pursue your spouse's military career and your own at an equal level as you move is tough, if not impossible. Hopefully, that will change as military moves become less frequent and as virtual positions and telecommuting make distance work more acceptable and available to spouses. For most of us, we make the choice that the military career is the lead and we manage to do what we can with our own careers as we move. In some situations, the couple chooses to ask for military assignments in locations that will benefit the civilian career as well. These decisions can sometimes limit the military member's long-term promotion potential. It's important to make these as conscious, joint decisions.

Other couples choose to have commuting marriages at certain times in order to allow the civilian spouse to continue in a great job or to accept a promotion that requires a move. Some couples make these commuting marriage decisions at times because of children's schooling considerations as well. We've talked with many spouses who have chosen the commuting life for a year or more. Most have said that, although they know it was the right thing for them to do at the time, it's a tough decision to make, especially considering the many separations already built into military life. They wouldn't recommend that choice if you can avoid it.

There are ways to pursue meaningful work that allow you to grow your skills with each move.

The good news is, there are ways to pursue meaningful work that allow you to grow your skills with each move. And it's crucial that you do that if work is one of your priorities. Once again, remember the research. It isn't achieving your career goal that brings the joy—it's the fact that you identify what interests you and you work to achieve it—in some manner. In some cases, the end result is more enriching than that straight-line path you can't take, even if it doesn't feel like it at the time.

Kathie's Story

As a brand new military wife at Fort Rucker, Alabama, I got my resume together and started clipping want ads every day. There weren't that many in rural Alabama. After months of searching, the best job opportunity I could find was selling vacuum cleaners door-to-door, hardly what I'd gone to college for and not something I wanted to do.

My second plan was to go for my MBA or law degree, only neither one was offered anywhere nearby.

> *I saw that assignment, that particular location, as empty of possi-*
> *bilities . . . as a dead-end to my dreams.*
>   *That was in 1978. Knowing what I know now, I realize that that*
> *location was full of possibilities—of opportunities. I just didn't know*
> *where to look and how to go about finding them. No one had ever*
> *taught me anything about job finding or goal-setting or possibility*
> *thinking. Plus, I was trying to do the job search all by myself, the least*
> *effective way to do one.*

In fact, many military spouses pursue their career the way that Kathie did—the least effective way. With each new duty station, Kathie found jobs based on the suggestions of others (without any further research into that field) or based on newspaper want ads—in other words, based on whatever was most easily available. She hopped from career field to career field, from human resources to pharmaceutical sales to advertising sales to advertising agency work.

So what's wrong with career hopping? Sure, it is one way to try out different things to find out what you like and don't like, but it's the least effective and most costly way. More important, when you keep changing career fields, you don't build up credentials and a reputation in any one field, you don't build connections that can help you as you move, and you are constantly in the beginner mode of the learning curve. It's hard to move up progressively position and salary-wise when you are continually starting over. After interviewing military spouses from all services, we've found many spouses are much more strategic in their career path. Lynn Edwards, an Army spouse, is a great example. We'll use her story as one example of this strategic path along with giving added examples from other spouses. As you read this consider how the strategies that worked for them might work for you, no matter what career field you want to pursue.

First, Know What You Want

Many of us skip the first and most important step in any effective job search. That is taking the time—and, yes, doing the work—to really figure out what it is we want to do. Many of us simply "fall" into careers based on others' suggestions, based on the money involved, the limits of "what we know to be available," or the jobs we find listed in the newspaper want ads.

If instead you factor in your values, skills, preferred work characteristics (and those you know you don't want), you're more likely to find a lasting fit.

Besides, knowing what you want makes for a more focused and effective job search as you move.

Lynn did the interest and values analysis to find a career field that fit her. "I'd always been about fun," she says. "I loved being involved with planning the prom, helping create school fundraisers, coordinating silent auctions. I've always been the one to plan get-togethers for my group of friends." She took a Recreation 101 course in college. As the professor described the ideal recreation professional—outgoing, organized, and so on—as well as the types of jobs available, Lynn thought to herself, "This is Julie on the Love Boat—I'm all about that!" She graduated with a degree in leisure studies. When she ended up married to the military, it turned out that working in the hospitality industry was one of the best career fields she could have chosen for this new lifestyle.

As she points out, no matter where you move with the military, there are hotels, tour companies, convention centers, resorts, event facilities, golf courses that do large events, and (of course) military morale, welfare, and recreation (MWR) opportunities.

Complete the Assessment/Interest Inventories and Pay Attention to Them

Cheryl Vollmer, an Air Force spouse, has worked with family members and service members for more than twenty years at Air Force Family Support Centers in Germany and the United States She recommends you check out the resources available right on base as a good starting point. "Check with your Family Support Center (Air Force), Army Community Service Center or Navy Service Center for individual assistance with the assessment tools they have available," says Cheryl. "The Air Force has a program called 'Discover' for example." She also recommends checking with the Education Center and on-base library. Many of the resources and assessment tools you would have to pay to access in the civilian world are available for free or at a lower cost through the military. But you have to take action to access them, and then be sure to pay attention to the results as you consider jobs. How does each career field or job fit your interests and skills?

We had considered including a long list of self-assessment web sites here. However, websites change so frequently, we recommend that you check with your family resource center to see what is current. Here are just a few to be aware of.

- Both military.com/spouse and militaryspousejobsearch.com have assessment tools for different career fields.

- Edgar Schein's book, *Career Anchors: Discovering Your Real Values,* includes assessment tools and interview questions to have a friend or family member ask you.
- The "guru" of career planning is Richard Bolles, author of the job search classic, *What Color is Your Parachute?*, which is updated regularly. His site (www.jobhuntersbible.com) is full of articles, assessment tools, and other resources.

Invest Time in Information Interviews

With the assessment results in hand, do a little more research on the fields and jobs you think you are most interested in. Conduct information interviews.

"The most powerful job search tool is the information interview," contends Rosemary Barnhart, a twenty-year career planning and employment consultant in Olympia, Washington. "You get ideas, make connections, get volunteer opportunities, and find great resources. You clarify in your mind whether or not this really is the job for you."

The idea is that, rather than judging a job or career path as appropriate for you just based on what you imagine about that job, talk to people doing that job to see if what you think matches reality. Gather information, learn the language, see how your skills fit in, make contacts, and determine your energy and enthusiasm for that career field—before you dive into a job search.

Let's consider air force spouse Stephanie, who is interested in becoming a paralegal. Who would she talk to and what would she ask? "I'd certainly suggest she talk to other paralegals," says Barnhart, "but she shouldn't limit herself to that." There are so many legal paraprofessionals, she goes on to say, from paralegals to lawyers to people who do legal research. Barnhart suggests talking to all of them to get a sense of the job and opportunities. There might be related positions Stephanie had never thought of or heard of—possibly positions that fit her skills, interests, and situation better. So, no matter what job you are interested in, think of related jobs where you might interview people for a bigger picture of what is available.

Why would someone grant you an information interview? "People love to talk about what they do—98.9 percent of people will say yes," says Barnhart.

As to what to ask, we have a more extensive list of possible questions on our website (militaryspousehelp.com) but here are a few to consider:

- What do you like best about what you do?
- What are your biggest challenges?
- What new and interesting things are happening in this field?
- What professional associations should I know about?

- What publications should I read?
- Are there opportunities for doing this kind of work virtually over the Internet?
- How might this fit into a mobile lifestyle?
- Are there opportunities in this career field across the country, in rural and urban settings, and overseas?

This powerful tool helps with career decisions as well as other life decisions. For example, if you are thinking about home schooling your children or taking on a volunteer position or creating a new program in your community to fill a need you see and care about, use the "information interview" format. Talk to others who are doing the same thing you want to do. Then make the decision with the facts instead of an imaginary image of what you think it might be like.

One in-depth way to research a career before undertaking it is to find an intern opportunity working for someone who does what you think you want to do. Or check out www.vocationvacations.com and see if you can "try out" your dream job before diving into a full-fledged job search for that career.

Know that you probably won't move in a straight line in your career—be open to that and adopt a mindset that opens you to possibilities. The reality of our military life is that you most likely won't move in a straight line upward in your career as you move with the military. With each move, Lynn has had a different kind of job within the industry. "Be open to that," she advises, "it deepens your experience and value." She's done unpaid internships in hotel sales. She's held jobs in recreation planning for MWR Korea, marketing for Sheraton Savannah Resort, sales for a historic inn, management for Yakima Valley Visitor's and Convention Bureau, convention sales for Ocean Shores Visitor's and Convention Bureau, and now does contract meeting planning, coordinating large events for clients like Microsoft and the NEC Invitational World Golf Championships. She's also creating her own dream, a business called FriendFest that brings girlfriends together at great resorts (check out www.friendfest.com), a culmination of all her skills and interests.

Join and Stay Active in Your Professional Association

Lynn has always been very involved with Meeting Planners International and the Society of Association Executives. "Your professional associations are hugely key," she advises, "especially moving internationally. The dues may seem high especially at first, but membership is worth its weight in gold."

Other spouses echo this idea. Amy Fetzer, marine spouse and romance author, belongs to the Author's Guild and Romance Writers of America. "Both organizations provided me with information I might not have found, especially since my writing took off when we lived in Okinawa before Internet connections were available." Cydnee, an educator, belongs to the National Educators Association and the National Association of Young Children. "My memberships have helped with resources and referrals," she says. Artist Kerry Vosler belongs to the Portrait Society of America and she joins all the art clubs in each area as she moves. "Your peers shorten your learning curve; they can save you a lot of time and money," says Kerry. "And with your association," she adds, "you have access to the famous people in your field; you get to talk to them at conferences."

Another great thing about belonging to your professional association is that you keep running into your peers at events even as you move nationally and internationally. Where you won't be able to keep your actual office mates in a job as you move, you can stay in touch with the larger "family" of your profession. With members all over the world, you always have someone to connect with when you move to a new location—and it's an easy connection to make.

Get Your Professional Certification

"I looked at the jobs I wanted five years down the road and asked what those folks did to get there," Lynn says. "In my world, it's the Certified Meeting Planner or CMP. It gives you instant credibility." Whereas most of us as military spouses feel we have to reestablish our credibility and professionalism with each move and each job, professional certification helps cut through that.

Personal trainer Phyllis Ward, army spouse, knows that her certification through the American Council on Exercise is key to her being seen as a professional. Elaine, the nurse, echoes that. "I see myself as competing [again after] every move and I position my skills and knowledge to help that competition." She chose to get a master's degree in business and a quality certification to make herself more competitive. And she made sure she took computer courses to keep her computer skills up to date, something necessary in the healthcare world of today and something that many nurses don't do. "You have to go beyond the minimum required for your state re-licensure if you want to position yourself to compete." Educator Cydnee agrees. "You have to have a lot of flexibility and multiple certifications. As the marines say, Semper Gumby, Always Flexible."

Look for Mentors, Negotiate Career-Building Opportunities, and Be Proactive on Cross Training

"You have to create your own opportunities," says Lynn. "Speak up and take things on." When she worked at the Yakima Convention and Visitors Bureau, for example, she said to her boss, "I'm not interested in your job since we'll be moving, but I want to learn." He let her sit in on Board Meetings and City Council Meetings. When her boss told her they couldn't afford to give her the raise she deserved, she negotiated time off and the entry fee to do her CMP training.

Start early in your job search and be persistent

When she found out they were moving to Savannah, Lynn got the event facilities list from the Convention and Visitors Bureau (CVB) and sent a cover letter and resume to every business listed there before she moved. Then she called those businesses, asking for information interviews and an opportunity to discuss the industry in that community. Once they arrived in Savannah, she went to CVB luncheons and stood up to say, "I'm new here and bring a wide skill set," handing out lots of cards. Even though she was frustrated that she didn't find something immediately, she says, "I did stuff every day—calls, meetings that forced me to get dressed, and I toured Savannah to get the lay of the land."

Army spouse Linda Beougher echoes the idea of starting your search early, as soon as you find out where you are moving—and of tapping into your current network to do so. When Linda and her husband arrived at Fort Leavenworth, Kansas, after their cross-country trip from Fort Lee, Virginia, she found an exciting message waiting for her. A Kansas City bank wanted to interview her for a current opening in investments. One week later, before they even received their household goods shipment, Linda started work, a short four weeks after leaving her banking job in Richmond. How did she do that? "In my job in Richmond, I traded funds all over the United States. So I asked everyone I traded with whom they might know in the Kansas area and specifically whom I should talk to and whom I should send my resume to." Networking resulted in the right contact. Linda's follow-through on that lead resulted in the interview.

Some Other Suggestions on Starting Before the Move:

- Update your resume and gather letters of recommendation. Put together a portfolio of successful projects and performance appraisals. This is much easier to do before you move and preparing ahead pays off. (By the way, Elaine recommends that you keep a running list of all employers with contact information. "One place checked my references ten jobs back," she reports.)
- Order the Chamber of Commerce information packet (free) and a membership directory (fee) for information on the companies in the area, the types of business, and number of employees, as well as contact information.
- Start a subscription to local business publications to read and clip files on companies that interest you (or read these online). You'll find information

on contracts, problems, and new projects. (This is part of the research you should do for any interview anyway.)

- Look for job search references specific to the area you are moving to. For example, if you are moving to the Seattle area there is *How to Find a Good Job in Seattle (Seventh Edition)*, by Linda Carlson. The Job Bank books are similar, with twenty different titles such as *The Denver Job Bank* and *The Carolina Job Bank*. Check with your reference librarian for titles specific to your new home. Many companies now have their job openings on their websites.

- Make use of the great new websites specific to military spouses. The Military Spouse Career Center, at www.military.com/spouse, includes listings specific for military spouses from 108 employers including Ann Taylor, Bell South, and Procter and Gamble. At www.MilitarySpouseJob Search.org, at least twenty-one large companies offer positions (including Lockheed Martin, Merck and Co., Sprint, Dell, and others). At www.msccn.org (Military Spouse Corporate Career Network), you'll find job listings from companies such as Boeing and Trammel Crowe. At www.MilSpouse.org, you can search for jobs as well as find out information about specific career fields, from requirements to industry outlook. All of these are free to you and searchable by location and specialty.

- If you belong to a professional association, call the chapter in the new city. Ask to receive their newsletters and meeting announcements ahead of the move to start collecting names to contact. Ask if they have a job bank you can tap into.

- If you are a college graduate, contact your alumni association and ask if there is a chapter in the new city. Or use your alumni directory to identify individuals in the city. Alumni like to help fellow alumni.

- Most important, tell everyone you know where you are moving to and ask them if they know people there. It doesn't have to be someone in a hiring position or even someone who works in your line of work. You just need contacts. Those contacts may just know the person you need to talk with. (Plus, you just might make new friends in the new location in the process.) A Department of Labor survey showed that 48 percent of jobs are found through friends or relatives and 24 percent are found through direct contact with an employer—going and asking for a job. Networking and following up with leads is key.

Be willing to take a pay cut for new experience (or just to continue in your field in a smaller community)

In Savannah, Lynn accepted a pay cut to work in sales at a high-end facility. Six months later she was promoted to director of sales. It may feel like "one step forward and two steps back" at times, but continuing to work in your chosen career path, continuing to make contacts and connections, might just be worth it in the long run.

Be Prepared to Make Changes in the Kind of Work You Do

Some jobs in the hospitality industry, for example, do not allow family flexibility. But some do. When Lynn had her second child, she chose Convention and Visitors Bureau work that was 8 a.m. to 5 p.m. and negotiated three days a week of work instead of five. Later, wanting even more flexibility, she started her own consulting firm.

As Peggy Frede, air force spouse and long-time educator says, "Accept jobs that stretch you professionally. Take the opportunity of a forced move to learn and try new techniques and methods." Peggy kept her mind open about opportunities in her career field. "I am an educator," she says. "Notice I didn't say teacher." It's a mindset that opened her to opportunities outside traditional schools when jobs weren't available there. Peggy has done traditional teaching in schools, managed a retraining program at a computer learning center, and taught technology at a law firm.

Elaine Wilhelm-Hass, the nurse, took advantage of the many moves to provide her with a wider range of experience, adding to her resume and marketability as she moved. She has worked in many different aspects of nursing, from staff RN to operating room manager to director of surgical and parent/child services at a hospital to quality improvement director for a Tricare region to healthcare consulting work.

Clare Morris, an army spouse, applied the same open mind to use her writing and public relations skills in a variety of positions as she moved. She's worked in the West Point public affairs office; writing freelance for magazines and newspapers; doing copywriting for corporate clients; as a press secretary and media relations director for a congressman both in Washington, DC, and later commuting from Florida; and as a technical writer/editor for a company in Germany.

Learn to Sell What You Bring to an Employer

"I'd basically say 'Lucky you, I bring a unique set of skills to town,'" says Lynn. After all, you bring a wide experience of seeing how other businesses run things, often bringing in new ideas that can help an operation. You bring the strength of flexibility and being able to deal with change, not a common skill, but a necessary one in today's business world. You've most likely learned to work with individuals from all levels of society and from different states and countries. People skills like that are key to any position. Recognize and sell the value you bring.

As Elaine says, "At first, I lamented that I'd always be the 'new RN,' working all the weekends and holidays—but here's a secret! The *new* kid from out of state is often perceived as more clever or desirable than existing employees. I capitalized on that."

Cydnee carries a portfolio with performance appraisals and letters of recommendation from previous duty stations, including any certificates of recognition or accomplishment for volunteer positions.

By the way, don't underestimate the skills and experience you've gained from your volunteer positions. Kathie heard one friend say disparagingly of herself, "I haven't had a paid job in so long—I don't know how marketable I am." This came from a woman who is as professionally polished and organized as any paid professional Kathie's ever worked with and who has successfully run large programs and organizations of volunteers. But that attitude of "lesser than" can hurt you in an interview. As Kathie points out from her years as a corporate personnel manager, "It's essential to appear enthusiastic and self-confident in an interview." Recognize the value of the skills you have and practice if necessary to sell them effectively in an interview.

On a similar note, Peggy says, "In interviews, be up front about your transient lifestyle. Turn it into a plus. I emphasize the wide range of subjects I've taught as well as the range of ages. I point out the varied perspectives and input I can provide from that wide experience at other locations."

As Richard Bolles, author of the classic *What Color is Your Parachute?* says, "When people change jobs frequently, their learning curve accelerates. They get the chance to learn more—and in less time. If I have one job for two years, and I get bounced out of it, or I decide to leave and go to a new place,

> *Turn your transient lifestyle into a plus in interviews.*

I have to start learning new stuff—a whole new set of skills that I didn't need in my last job. This makes me a more valuable employee, wherever I go." Based on that, military spouses have to be some of the most valuable employees anywhere! Be aware of that and sell yourself accordingly.

Here's a partial list of the benefits military spouses bring to their employers:

- Ability to deal with change/flexibility,
- Ability to learn quickly,
- Ability to work with people from all walks of life,
- Ideas and experiences from many other companies and organizations,
- Strong people skills, and
- Global experience and familiarity with international customs.

Build Networking Skills to Make and Keep Great Connections

We can't emphasize this enough! "My industry is very incestual," says Lynn. "The management and sales jobs rarely make it into an ad. It's always through networking. It's who you know who knows how well you work!"

As Phyllis, the personal trainer says, "I joined the Cheyenne Mountain Newcomers Club for networking and it has been one of my best sources for clients." Ann Strand, army spouse and a Pampered Chef director, says, "I volunteer in my community. I associate with others and then they want to have shows. It is how my business grows; every new booking brings more."

It's who you know who knows how well you work!"

By the way, if you are not a natural networker, check out the books by Anne Baber and Lynn Waymon in our resource list. It is a skill anyone can learn.

Create your own visibility—learn the art of personal PR and marketing yourself. Lynn volunteers to speak and teach classes on the leisure industry for community colleges, universities, and at conferences. She has volunteered time on the boards of the state chapters of her professional associations.

All of these strategies will work with any industry.

One added thought: What if you do the skills and interest inventories, and still don't know what you really want to do? Well, then, look at this military life as a true gift as you get the opportunity to try new jobs/careers on for size with each move. We both know plenty of civilian friends who continue unhappily in jobs they've been at for twenty years just because they are too afraid to make a change. Sometimes forced change is good.

Can't the Services Help Us with This?

The services know that mobile careers for spouses are a key factor in keeping us happy, which means better retention rates for our spouses. It costs money to constantly recruit and retrain new military members. It behooves the services to find ways to keep our spouses in—and one way is to keep us happy.

That's why the Department of Defense partnered with military.com and monster.com to create www.military.com/spouse, where military spouses can look for job openings and apply online, with the site's services free to spouses. The individual services continuously bring out new programs, from the Navy and Marine Adecco Career Accelerator (www.adecco.com) to the air force's Virtual Assistant Training program, which has been expanded to all services (www.staffcentrix.com) to the army's partnering with corporations to promote the value of army spouses for traditional, telework, and virtual positions (www.militaryspousejobsearch.org now available to spouses of all services).

The relatively new Spouses to Teachers program (www.spousestoteachers.org) helps to research the certification requirements by state as you move and will pay $600 toward your certification or recertification.

We're excited to hear about new programs. Tap into them all. Realize, however, that successfully transferring your career or business and finding work at each location still comes down to a lot of personal initiative, creativity, and flexibility.

So access those services available through the military. And access others. As Janet Farley, author of *Jobs and the Military Spouse,* says, "Use the services available to you on the military installation, but also take advantage of those services offered within the civilian community outside the front gate. For example, register with the Department of Labor (DoL) and inquire about the availability of unemployment benefits. Laws are always changing in this area and if you are eligible for this benefit, use it. Aside from that, the DoL is well plugged into the community and will refer you, free of charge, to employers." (Note: currently twenty-six states offer unemployment benefits to military spouses who have to leave jobs because of a military move, so check that out.) In some states, workforce training dollars are available for spouse education and training. Ask!

Network with other military spouses to help with job searches as you move. With 65 percent of military spouses working, and all of us moving frequently, there seems a great possibility of referring each other for positions and providing a service to our current employers at the same time. According to the Department of Labor, the number one challenge for business growth in the United States is the need for skilled workers. Partner that with the fact that 43 percent of military spouses are underemployed, and you have a perfect situation for a match-up that will be a win/win all around.

And as Kathie can tell you from her years as a corporate personnel manager, she always preferred referrals from good employees who already know the corporate environment. Think about it: we network with others to find out where to have our hair cut or our car fixed. If we more effectively tap into the network of close to one million military spouses, we can help each other find good jobs and help our employers find good workers. In addition, tap into military.com/spouse's networking feature.

Also access information and resources that are out there for other "trailing spouses" such as expatriate spouses and foreign service spouses. Books such as Nancy Mueller's *Work Worldwide: International Career Strategies for the Adventurous Job Seeker,* and Frances Bastress's *The New Relocating Spouses Guide to Employment: Options in the U.S. and Abroad* are full of great ideas and resources that can work for military spouses as well as you move overseas.

What if *No* Job is Available in Your Career Field with This Move?

It happens. You move with the military and what you want to do is simply not available at that location. What do you do? Give up? Settle for a career field you aren't excited about? Take a job, any job? Unfortunately, that is what many of us do. Yes, sometimes financially you have no choice but to do so. If you can manage without a paycheck for a time, however, another idea would be to see if you can find or create the job you want via volunteer work. If that isn't possible, identify the skills you need for your dream job—be it computer, marketing, managing others, fund-raising, PR—and find volunteer work to teach you those skills.

LaMuir Baze gave up on college for herself when she married a sailor. Since her husband was an E1 there was no money for college courses. She started looking for work to fit a mobile lifestyle and ran across an advertisement for the American Red Cross, looking for spouses to volunteer at the dental clinic. Volunteering 225 hours earns a certificate of completion to be a certified dental sssistant.

"Since my training with the Red Cross," LaMuir says, "I've been able to work in four states and qualified for the National Boards while working for Dental Command in New York." LaMuir took some time off to spend with her now five-year-old quadruplets. She's back at work now for extra income and "a sanity break for mommy."

"I've been blessed to have this opportunity," she adds, "I've been able to support my husband in his military career, from starting as an E1 in the Navy to being a CW2 in the Army as a Blackhawk Pilot. What other job would give me the flexibility to start and stop when I needed to in order to meet the needs of my family?"

Sarah Selvidge, an army spouse, wanted to work in marketing, so she volunteered at the Bamberg Germany community marketing office to learn the ropes. She later worked as a marketing manager for World Vision in Seattle.

Samantha wanted to own her own pet resort. She first volunteered at her community's vet clinic and was eventually hired at the vet clinic at her next location, giving her the opportunity to keep learning the ropes—and building her credibility—before she puts her own money and time into her pet resort.

Kathie built her speaking and writing business this way, taking volunteer positions using those skills in order to develop the skills and to develop her portfolio. She used a regular column for the Fort Lewis Wives Club newsletter followed by the Heidelberg Wives Club newsletter as stepping stones to continued writing. Those experiences gave her the courage to try for paid articles and columns. She could say to an editor, "I've had to meet monthly deadlines for more than three years and have never missed a deadline," something important to selling an editor on your work. And she had samples of published work to show.

What if you have to earn a living—have to take some job? Well, then apply the same concept to your job search. When you can't find a job in your specific career field, at least be selective in what is available. Rather than just taking any job, look for a job that allows you to learn or improve on skills you need in your chosen career. On the job, ask for opportunities to take on projects or training to enhance those skills.

We have one advantage now as military spouses that did not exist in the past. In the past, many companies would actually say, "We don't hire military wives," or want ads would read "local only need apply." Many of us in the past found ourselves having to hide the fact that we were military spouses. We had to be extra creative to explain our spotty resumes. That has changed. Companies are now used to people changing jobs frequently. It's become the norm in the civilian world too. In fact, the average American will change jobs eleven times in a forty-year career. There is no longer such a stigma about having a resume with lots of different jobs listed. Remember to turn all that experience into a strength, and into a benefit for your new employer. Sell yourself!

The bottom line reality is that you probably won't have the steady, straight-line career path that your nonmilitary peers may be able to manage. And that may be the best thing that ever happened to you!

As Janet Farley, military spouse and author adds, "If you can't find the job of your dreams at your next duty station, use the opportunity for what it is . . . an opportunity to try something new. You never know, you just might latch onto your true calling, compliments of a set of orders you weren't too thrilled with in the first place."

Lynn says, "I doubt that I'd have had the guts or the wide range of skills necessary to start my own consulting business and the FriendFest program if I'd stayed in one place."

Army spouse Berkeley McHugh has had some fabulous opportunities because of moving around and teaching at different schools. "I went back to Texas ten years after I first taught there," she says, "and many of my former coworkers were still there, teaching the same subject in the same room. I feel that I had additional opportunities to grow and be challenged because of my new environments."

Peggy says, "I have a variety of great experiences that I wouldn't trade for a thirty-year career in any school district!" We hope you end up saying the same, whatever career you pursue.

Resources

Department of Defense has a contract with military.com and monster.com; www.military.com/spouse

Jobs and the Military Spouse: Married, Mobile and Motivated for Employment (Second Edition), by Janet I. Farley (2004)

Make Your Contacts Count, by Anne Baber and Lynne Waymon (2002)

Great information and tips, tools and techniques on networking. There are other useful resources at their website (www.contactscount.com)

Militaryspousejobsearch.org for job listings, assessment tools and career information

Mobile Career Article Series. We write a column for *Military Money* magazine on career fields that tend to be more mobile: education, hospitality industry, healthcare, government agencies, contract work, writing, and many others. For archived articles, check out www.militarymoney.com or our website, militaryspousehelp.com

What Color is Your Parachute? by Richard Bolles (2004); www.jobhunters bible.com

VocationVacations at www.vocationvactions.com, or 1-866-888-6329

Work Worldwide: International Career Strategies for the Adventurous Job Seeker, by Nancy Mueller (2000)

Career Anchors: Discovering Your Real Values, by Edgar Schein [1985, rev.2006] page 94.

The Military Spouses' Corporate Career Network (www.msccn.org)

The New Relocating Spouses Guide to Employment: Options in the U.S. and Abroad, by Frances Bastress (1993)

Spouse employment services on your installation:

Army Employment Readiness Program

Air Force Career Focus Program

Navy Spouse Employment Assistance Program

Marine Family Member Employment Assistance

Chapter 9

Wouldn't It Be Easier to Have My Own Business?

Moving a Business as You Move

Some military spouses choose to create their own business. It's something they can move with them, rather than constantly going through a job search with each move. It's something they can continue to build as they move, with an eye to expanding it even more once they stop moving.

Is a business right for you? There are a lot of things to consider in setting up any business. Setting one up that you have to move every few years raises additional considerations.

This is a huge topic to try to cover in one chapter. But we wanted to give you some things to think about and some resources to refer to if you are considering a business.

The Realistic News

Statistics aren't promising. U.S. Small Business Administration statistics indicate that one-third of new businesses fail within two years; half fail within four years, and 60 percent fail within six years. Lest you think that magic "if you make it through the first five, you've made it" myth is true, Michael Gerber reports in his book, *The E-Myth Revisited: Why Most Small Businesses Don't Work and What to Do About It,* that 80 percent of businesses that survive the first five years fail in the second five.

According to Sharon Barber, assistant district director for Tacoma's Small Business Administration office, there are two key reasons why small businesses fail. The first is under capitalization, not having enough working funds. This is often caused by not doing a business plan ahead of time. A business plan helps you to have realistic expectations of what your business will require in funding and what is possible. The second reason is poor management. "Many people have the skills to do the creative or production part of their business," she says. Where they fall down is in the accounting and management side that every business requires as well.

We don't know what the statistics are for businesses run by military spouses, but we know that those businesses face added challenges when you factor in frequent moves and other aspects of military life.

Can You Make Money Right Away?

Many of us who start businesses have the misguided idea that we can start making money at it right away. Now, that might be true in some cases. For example, if you work for a corporation and they agree to contract with you to do that same work as an independent contractor, you probably can start to make money immediately. Some virtual assistant businesses show profits from the start. But for most of us, that isn't the case.

Many of the spouses we've talked to, ourselves included, will tell you that they've had mixed experiences with the financial side of their businesses. As one woman describes her experience only half jokingly, "When I took this business on, I didn't realize I was taking on a major volunteer position in a nonprofit endeavor." One woman's husband calls her business her "most expensive hobby." Many spouses admit that they would not have the bravery to try their own business if they didn't have their spouses' income and benefits as the stable base to allow them to take time to grow the business.

There are a lot of start-up costs for any business, from business equipment and supplies to business stationery to phone-line hookups. Even the simplest of businesses has expenses. Realize that many of those costs reoccur with each move, as you have to file your business in the new state and pay for new phone hookups and new business cards.

When you have your own business, you have monthly overhead costs, expenses that recur whether or not you are actively doing business or bringing in income. For example, your monthly telephone bill, Internet service provider, and web hosting fees arrive each month without fail.

If starting your own business is about the money, and not about passion, or at least about the flexibility, you might want to think again. As Barry Moltz says in *You Need to Be a Little Crazy: The Truth about Starting and Growing Your Business,* "Make no mistake; it is easier and in the long run more profitable to get a job than to start your own business."

Where Will You Get Your Customers or Clients?

Successful businesses are built on client relationships and referrals. One consideration for us as military spouses in looking at a business is whether or not those referrals will work across the country and the world.

For someone in a network marketing business such as Pampered Chef or Nikken or Heritagemaker Books, referrals and repeat business can move with you. For a speaker or trainer, your referrals and repeat business can also move, as long as you have access to the Internet and to a major airport and clients willing to pay travel expenses. For a writer or virtual assistant, all you need is a telephone and Internet connection. The important thing to consider before starting any business is how moving might impact your current and future client base.

> *One important thing to consider before starting any business is how moving might impact your current and future client base.*

Are You Ready to Do It All?

Many of us start businesses doing things that we love and are good at. The challenge is that as a small business owner, you also undertake many other tasks just to stay in business. These may *not* be things you love to do or are good at—activities such as accounting, tax preparation, marketing, sales, data entry, pricing, proposal preparation, invoicing, customer service, record keeping, understanding and abiding by government regulations, purchasing, order fulfillment, calling for overdue payments—all have to be taken care of. If you don't do them, you have to pay someone else to do them. Most small business owners don't start out with enough money to pay anyone else.

As Michael Gerber says in *The E-Myth,* "The business that was supposed to free him from the limitations of working for somebody else actually enslaves him. Suddenly the job he knew how to do so well becomes one job he knows how to do plus a dozen others he doesn't know how to do at all."

Do You Have What It Takes, or, Are You Cut Out for Entrepreneurship?

It's a good idea to approach a new business the way you would a new career field. Do the research. Conduct information interviews with those who have successful businesses to find out what it takes and what the possibilities are. If you don't do some research and apply some solid business practices, you may end up with the situation described by Gerber, a situation many small business owners find themselves in after a few years.

"You one day realize," Gerber says, "You don't own a business, you own a job! What's more it's the worst job in the world! You can't close it when you want to, because if it's closed you don't get paid. You can't leave it when you want to, because when you leave, there is nobody there to do the work. You can't sell it when you want to, because who wants to buy a job?"

It's important to be honest with yourself about your work habits and skills and how those might translate into business management. Are you organized, detail-oriented, good with follow through, and self-directed?

Probably the two most important attributes are the ability to network/connect with others, and the ability to sell. As Moltz says, "Only sales will build your business . . . if you are afraid to sell, you have two choices: You can get over it or get a job."

How Will This Affect Your Family?

There is the time and family balance issue. If you aren't careful, the business can take over your life. As Janelle Davis says, "The key advantage to a virtual business is staying home with my daughter and setting my own hours . . . and the main challenge of this business is working at home with my daughter." Other home-based business owners echo this. As virtual assistant Charlotte says, "My biggest challenge is being able to balance my time so that my work does not take over all of my time with my kids . . . the main reason I decided to stay home."

Home-based businesses do provide flexibility, but they also require lots of organization skills, self-discipline, and family understanding.

Some Good News and Success Stories

Many spouses turn to network marketing companies such as Longaberger Baskets or Arbonne or Polish Stoneware at Home to start a business. These companies provide a ready-made product, training, and assistance to help you succeed. You don't have to figure things out and create everything from scratch. Although you are still a one-person operation, you have the support and camaraderie of other distributors and the specific help of your director.

Ann Strand, an Army spouse, finds this kind of business perfect for her after trying other career and business avenues. Plus, with young children at home, this kind of business offers the flexibility of schedule she wanted. In 2002, she earned top honors as one of Pampered Chef's best recruits and is currently a director working out of Oklahoma.

"This business involves my whole family," adds Ann. "My children have learned goals, learned healthy eating, and learned about achieving dreams."

Is a network marketing/direct sales business for everyone? Of course not. So much of it depends on how you work it. We've heard of spouses making more in their network marketing business than their military spouses made in salary and benefits. We can also share stories of spouses who spent more money than they ever made in a network marketing business.

Hope Larson is an army spouse and a real estate broker with RMI (RE/MAX International). RMI is one company that offers employment to military spouses worldwide. In 2006, they kicked off Operation RE/MAX, an initiative to hire military spouses and provide ongoing support, as Realtors® or in administrative support positions. Hope was Rookie of the Year for her area in 2005, grossing $80,000 in ten months' time.

"One fifth of my income comes from relocation referrals," she says. "The referral piece is critical as it is the most mobile part of my business—and it allows me flexibility." She connects military families or others moving to a new location to a RMI agent who fits their needs. In exchange she typically earns a 25 percent referral fee. "Even if I move from my current location, my clients in Maryland can still call me to refer them to an agent. Why pick me? Because we have established a trust and I stay on top of the situation from start to finish to ensure they receive the best service available." She can also turn to referral work when her husband's deployment requires more time flexibility in her life.

Evy Packard-Williams is an army spouse with a master's degree in administration who focuses her virtual assistant business, BrochuresByDesign.com, on marketing, desktop publishing, and professional writing services. After years in the corporate world, she appreciates the flexibility this business provides. "I love being able to take the time my family needs and work when I can. I can work early in the morning or late at night if I have to."

The Virtual Advantage

The Internet has opened up incredible opportunities for us as military spouses who want to own a business. The Internet allows us to have a website and email address that stays the same as we move from place to place, so our customers and prospects can easily find us. That wasn't the case in the past, as we had to change contact information with each move.

As army spouse, mother, and freelance writer Regina Galvin told us after one move, "I have enough work lined up in advance that I can keep the momentum going with this upcoming move—as long as I have my laptop with me."

With the introduction of email, we can now afford to conduct business as we move either long distance and overseas—something formerly cost-prohibitive when we were limited to expensive long-distance telephone calls. And, of course, we can conduct our business at all hours, which helps with our life schedules as military spouses. The high quality computers and printers available today allow small businesses more flexibility than in the past. Many people don't bother to have new stationery or marketing materials printed anymore, choosing instead to simply print them off as needed from color printers. In some businesses, print materials are unnecessary as the website serves as the marketing vehicle. That saves time and money to military spouses as we move our businesses and change our focus and offerings.

Virtual Businesses Today Can Cover a Wide Range of Specialties

Air Force spouse Charlotte Lingard-Young's business, C.Y. Virtual Solutions, puts her background in healthcare and master's degree in applied psychology to work for her clients doing Internet research and general and psychiatric transcription among other services.

Army spouse Jeri Winkler combines a computer science degree with real estate experience in her virtual business called The Secret Assistant. She provides Realtors® with everything from database management to prospecting to website maintenance. Her familiarity with popular real estate software programs allows her to handle time-consuming office tasks from a distance.

Air Force spouse Janelle Davis combines a law degree and experience in commercial litigation and appeals to provide motion and brief preparations for her clients.

As Chris Durst, who is credited with founding the Virtual Assistance (VA) industry in 1995 points out, VAs are home-based entrepreneurs who run their own shows offering business support services to other businesses via email, phone, and fax. Durst and Michael Haaren, cofounders of Staffcentrix, have trained, taught, or mentored more than thirty-eight hundred VAs internationally. In their book, *The Two-Second Commute: Join the Exploding Ranks of Freelance Virtual Assistants,* they identify more than eighty varieties of expertise, ranging from basic word processing to high-end corporate consulting.

Many specialties listed in their book seem tailor-made for the background and experience of military spouses: event planning, expertise in foreign markets, interpreting, import/export support, nonprofit support services, government procurement expertise, resume writing, fundraising.

Staffcentrix's program "The Portable Career and Virtual Assistance Training Program™" geared specifically to military spouses kicked off with a pilot at Cannon AFB in 2002. Since then Staffcentrix has provided programs to many other military sites. Their "Train the Trainer" program certifies spouse employment professionals from all services. More than thirty-one hundred military spouses are now part of the Military Spouse Virtual Assistant community.

If you think about it, any business that a military spouse runs and moves from location to location is a virtual business.

Businesses That Develop by Chance and Serendipity—And Because of—Military Life

Some spouses fall into business opportunities, often owing to adversity or from seeing a need that needs filling, or simply from experiences they have because of military life.

Ellie Kay is married to an air force pilot and is mother to a family of seven. She weathered eleven moves in thirteen years and dealt with deployments. Ellie wanted to stay home with her children and get rid of their family's $40,000 debt, so she had no choice but to draw on her business background and learn how to handle her family finances in a masterful way. She became so good at it that she started giving volunteer "Shop, Save, and Share" seminars to other military families at their local base. Her seminars came to the attention of Lenn Furrow, director of the Family Support Center at Holloman Air Force Base. Lenn approached the Air Force Aid Society to fund a film project based on the seminars. That became a video distributed to 120 air force bases worldwide.

Serendipity stepped in and the seminar came to the attention of a literary agent, who took it to the senior editor at Bethany House Publishers, which resulted in Ellie's first book, *Shop, Save, and Share.* The success of that book quickly led to two others, *How to Save Money Every Day,* and *Money Doesn't Grow on Trees.* She later wrote *Heroes at Home* for military families, which became a 2003 Gold Medallion Book Award finalist. Her business has grown. She is a regular guest on CNBC's Power Lunch, a spokesperson for corporations such as Visa, MasterCard, and HealthInsurance.com and a national radio commentator for Money Matters.

Army spouse Tara Crooks decided to switch from her customer service job in retail management to Mary Kay cosmetic sales because she "wanted her own thing." In the process she taught herself web design and opened a candle business, which she later sold for a profit. As she started focusing on marketing and advertising for moms in business, she happened to be interviewed numerous times on WorkingMomTalkRadio.com. The host suggested she should have her own talk show. That triggered ArmyWifeTalkRadio.com, which Tara started at home while her husband was deployed to Iraq. A year and fifty-two shows later, she's found her passion and has lots of plans for expansion with ebooks, books, other talk shows, and public speaking opportunities ahead. Also, her shows are loaded with information useful to spouses of all services.

Lorna Dupuoy spent ten years as a marine herself, and then married into the navy. As a navy spouse for eighteen years, she did a variety of jobs, including teaching at the high school level and acting as general manager for a family theme park in Virginia Beach. Since her husband had three commands over that time, she also spent a lot of time organizing functions and entertaining. "I always loved people and parties and events," she says, "Now I'm going to do the same thing and get paid for it." As her husband approaches retirement, they are pursuing her dream business. They invested in a big, old, white house behind a long stonewall fence in the resort area of Saratoga Springs, New York, where Lorna grew up. She's creating two businesses at that location: an event/ retreat center named Villeroy along with an etiquette school.

Many military spouses have gravitated to the professional organizing business. "I moved a household of three kids twelve times, both in this country and to foreign countries," says Michelle Walsh. "I also helped organize a variety of different offices over the years. That all gave me solid experience to teach others." Vicky Harding moved twenty-seven times. "I learned quickly that I didn't want the move to consume my time, so I figured out systems that worked." She helps others develop systems. Her years of volunteer training with Red Cross, ACS, and the Army Family Action Plan (AFAP) gave her skills she needed to run her own workshops as part of her business.

The Bottom Line

Some spouses told us that they learned by doing that running a business was not for them. However, as they all pointed out, if they hadn't tried they would always have wondered and probably lived with regrets.

Some businesses have done well in some locations and faltered during other moves and economic upheavals. Some of the business owners we talked with are simply happy to see forward progress with each move and fully expect the profit situation to improve dramatically only when they stop moving and can stabilize the business. However, many of these still say they are happy they've been moving a business rather than searching for a job with each move. They are doing work they love, building something for the future, enjoying more flexibility than they might otherwise, and have tax write-offs for much of what they do.

Kathie's Story

If I had it all to do over again, would I start a business? Well, I have mixed answers to that. On the one hand, I know I would have made way more money by continuing to take jobs with each move, as well as building up more on the Social Security side of the ledger toward retirement. There are many times, quite honestly, when I'm simply overwhelmed by everything that needs to be done in a business, when I know it would be easier to have a job with a guaranteed paycheck and vacation days, and with no need to constantly market myself and my business.

I've had good years and bad years financially with this business. One thing that has stayed constant, however, is the deep satisfaction that I get from doing the research, writing, program development, and presentations. I may not enjoy aspects of being a business owner, but I love the core work I do. I love the opportunity to constantly learn new things I'm interested in learning.

The business has allowed me flexibility that kept our life sane with moves and deployments. It allowed me to fully use my own creativity and to do work that I love that actually makes a difference. It allowed me to spend time and money on many things I would have wanted to spend time and money on anyway, from attending workshops to buying books, valid tax-deductible business expenses instead of personal expenses. It's allowed me to develop skills and strengths and self-confidence that I can carry into any new endeavor. And I've had experiences I wouldn't give up for anything.

If I knew then what I know now, I would certainly do many things differently as I built the business. I would have taken business classes right up front, to really learn about small business taxes and legalities. I would have done up a business plan and worked with the Small Business Administration and with the SCORE program's free advice. I would have set up a board of advisors, of people with the skills that I lack that are important to business development. I would have started out by volunteering to apprentice with an established speaker, to learn the ropes and make good contacts as I helped them develop their business. If I'd done that for free or low pay even, I could have learned what I needed to know without first spending my own money to do so, and most likely made valuable connections at the same time. I might have looked for a job or volunteer position like AFTB where I could learn the skills and get paid training rather than spending my own money on that kind of training.

The bottom line for me is that I do want to continue to build and grow both my writing and speaking, and to create a successful business that I can continue late into life. I'm thankful now that this military life led me to this work I love, something that might not have happened if I'd stayed in one place working in one career field.

Staffcentrix tracked the outcome of the military spouse virtual assistant training through quarterly reports from all military spouses who attend training in 2004. Eighty-nine percent of spouses who launched a VA business reported improved quality of life. Isn't that what our life choices are all about?

Resources

Making a Living Without a Job, by Barbara Winter (1993). Full of great stories and inspiration for those of us looking to have a small one-person business. We find her ideas of having "multiple profit centers" key to what we do. Barbara also has a great print newsletter called *Winning Ways* that Kathie has been getting for fourteen years now. "It's one of the few things I read cover to cover when it arrives in the mail," she says. Also, see www.barbarawinter.com.

The E-Myth Revisited: Why Most Small Businesses Don't Work and What to Do About It, by Michael Gerber (1995).

Make Your Contacts Count: Networking Know-How for Cash, Clients, and Career Success, by Anne Baber and Lynne Waymon, and additional resources at their website, www.contactscount.com.

www.military.com/careers/spouses.html. This useful site covers what to consider when starting a business and where to get information.

www.military.com/operationRemax/REMAX.htm.

Working from Home: Everything You Need to Know About Living and Working Under the Same Roof, Fifth edition, by Paul and Sarah Edwards (1999).

Working Solo: The Real Guide to Freedom and Financial Success with Your Own Business, Second edition, by Terri Lonier (1998).

You Need to Be a Little Crazy: The Truth about Starting and Growing Your Business, by Barry J. Moltz (2003). From a "serial entrepreneur" with both failures and successes in various businesses, full of lots of quotes and stories from the trenches showcasing the realities rather than the fantasies of owning your own business.

Resources for Virtual Assistants:

International Virtual Assistants Association—www.ivaa.org

REVA Network (Real Estate Virtual Assistants)—www.revanetwork.com

Staffcentrix—www.staffcentrix.com (includes the Military Spouse Virtual Assistants group)

Work-the-Web.com—www.work-the-web.com

The Two-Second Commute: Join the Exploding Ranks of Freelance Virtual Assistants, by Christine Durst and Michael Haaren (and their new CD: *The*

Staffcentrix Home-Based Job Power Search, full of links for virtual business connections)

Military Spouse Businesses Mentioned Here:

Tara Crooks—ArmyWifeTalkRadio.com

Lorna Dupuoy—www.TheEtiquetteSchoolofNewYork.com

Ellie Kay—www.elliekay.com

Hope Larson—www.hopecan.com

Charlotte Lingard-Young, C.Y. Virtual Solutions—www.cyvirtualsolutions.com

Ann Strand—www.pamperedchef.biz/ubookanncooks

Jeri Winkler, The Secret Assistant—www.secretassistant.com

Chapter 10

To Volunteer or Not to Volunteer

Volunteering Your Time Has
Benefits and Challenges

Volunteering Connects You to the Military Community

Nada Walton arrived at Fort Lewis, Washington, as a new bride, moving to the United States from Montreal, Canada. She was entering a new country and a whole new world. "When I first got here, I knew nothing about the military," she said. "I knew nobody, and nobody knew me." It's an apt description for most of us as brand new military spouses. We know nothing about the military, we know nobody, and nobody knows us.

Another military spouse told Nada about the free program called Army Family Team Building (AFTB), a series of classes to teach spouses everything they need to know about this military life. After one class, Nada wanted to get involved. She started teaching classes, volunteering as briefing manager, and doing the monthly newsletter, spending from five to thirty hours a week volunteering. She became involved in other volunteer projects in activities that interested her, from helping create the Family Readiness Group for her husband's unit to helping with duathlon and triathlon competitions on post.

Nada talks about the sense of satisfaction she gets out of volunteering. She also describes the deep friendships she's developed. She's no longer alone. She is now part of a community of others going through what she's going through.

Our military communities and our quality of life are deeply dependent on volunteers. Volunteering can be a win/win opportunity. You make a difference, increase your own self-esteem and happiness, develop new skills, and connect with others. But volunteering has its challenges and sometimes can have a negative effect.

We have each experienced both ends of the spectrum with volunteering. We hear the same from many military spouses we talk to. We both started out in the "not involved and choosing not to be involved" group of military spouses. We were busy with careers and we resented the extreme expectations we encountered—the expectation that all military spouses should volunteer. We especially resented the fact that in those years, spouse involvement (or noninvolvement) was actually included on our husbands' military efficiency reports. That is no longer allowed, thank goodness.

That change came about through the actions of military spouses. Twenty years ago military wives were expected to volunteer but not to work for pay. In 1985, two air force colonels' wives spoke out, creating lots of adverse publicity. As a result, a subcommittee of the House Armed Services Committee interviewed wives in the United States and overseas and confirmed that wives had been told not to work. In 1987, the Department of Defense issued the Working Military Spouse Policy, Directive 1400.33. It stated that, "no DOD official, individual commanding officer or supervisor shall directly or indirectly, impede or otherwise interfere with the right of every military spouse to decide whether to pursue or hold a job, attend school or perform voluntary services on or off a military installation." Secretary of Defense Caspar W. Weinberger signed a letter on October 22, 1987, addressed to the secretaries of the military departments. The letter emphasized, "Spouses . . . have a right to seek employment, to be homemakers, or to volunteer for command-sponsored activities." He further stated that "no military member will be adversely rated or suffer any adverse consequences from the decision of the member's spouse to seek employment."

We hear from many spouses that, even though things have changed since the 1980s, in some cases expectations remain. It's the expectation that they "have to" volunteer that they resent. They resent the judgment of others if they don't choose to volunteer.

In our cases, we weren't interested in many of the things we were asked to do especially those during the workday when we couldn't participate even if we wanted to. The thing we didn't realize at the time was that by avoiding all opportunities to volunteer, we kept ourselves apart from the military community. When we had to go to unit functions we didn't know people. We felt awkward and uncomfortable at those functions. We were living a life separate from the lives of our spouses.

Eventually, we each chose to volunteer when we saw a need that we were interested in filling that fit our available time. It was our choice, not a requirement from anyone. The interesting thing for us was that those volunteer activities changed our experience of military life. We went from living on the outside to feeling connected and enriched—as well as feeling more of a partnership with our spouses.

Is volunteering the only way to feel connected to this world we are a part of? Of course not. We know military spouses who are fully connected with their neighbors on post or base, or through their work in a civil service position or teaching at a school on the military installation. Some of them do no volunteering in the military community. They choose instead to be involved with programs outside the military community, in their churches, or in national programs. Some have full lives without any volunteering at all. We just know that volunteering in the military community has been one avenue for many of us to connect quickly with this world. As with everything else, there is no one model of community involvement that works for everyone. You have to find what works best for you.

When we started volunteering we went from living on the outside to feeling connected and enriched.

We also know many spouses who live rich full lives without any real connection to the military world that their spouses are living in. They don't feel a need for any further connection. They've created their own support system outside the military. Our experience has been one that we hear echoed by many military spouses, however. When you are dealing with a deployment, you often have an easier time if you live on the military installation or at least connect regularly with other spouses dealing with deployment. There is the sense of camaraderie and the knowledge that so many others around you are dealing with the same thing. Off the military installation, you often feel as if the country has all but forgotten that your spouse is deployed and in danger. You can feel truly alone and forgotten.

As with everything else, there is no one model of community involvement that works for everyone.

Kathie's Story

I volunteered first to write a regular column for the Fort Lewis wives club newsletter—on fun things to do around Fort Lewis, Washington. It was a way to get connected, to help the editor out, to help other spouses explore this area, and to force myself to finally start writing as I kept saying I wanted to do.

I took over as editor of our family support group newsletter as a way to force myself to learn desktop publishing, something that has helped tremendously in my business. I've since been editor of many organization publications and continue to volunteer my writing services, both for military and nonmilitary groups.

I did free speaking for military spouse groups at Fort Lewis and McChord AFB for two years and then all over Europe for three years. That allowed me to provide a service and build my speaking skills and material while I connected to the community.

I now spend a lot of time one-on-one with other military spouses by email and telephone, brainstorming ways they can move toward what they want in life, sharing ideas, resources and contacts.

As you can tell, for the most part I choose to do things I can do at home and on my own schedule. I knew I wanted to build a business and didn't want to be tied to meetings and other people's schedules. My choice of volunteer projects allow me to fill a need, connect with others, be part of the community, and keep the flexibility that I want. It also gives me the chance to learn things I want to learn.

Holly's Story

From the day I started planning my wedding to Jack, I assumed I'd be going to Germany. I couldn't wait to go in fact! Ten years later, when we finally got to Bamberg, Germany, the reality was totally different from what I'd been visualizing.

I found myself in a foreign country living on a military installation and not wanting to venture outside the gates because of the unknowns and language barrier. Kathie had just moved to Heidelberg. She could tell how frustrated I was, so we got permission for me to attend Heidelberg's FLAG (Families Learning About Germany) orientation program, something the Bamberg community did not offer at the time. It made all the difference, giving me skills to survive.

I didn't want other spouses to go through what I'd gone through at first. So I joined forces with Bamberg's Family Advocacy program manager, Heather Reekie, to create an orientation program for Bamberg. I volunteered forty to sixty hours a week to co-create and market the new program called PEP: People Encouraging People. It was so successful; we ended up with waiting lists of people. We even presented briefings to other communities on how they could create a similar welcome program in their community. I was having a ball, and getting fully connected with this community. I was energized by what I was doing.

The best thing was it made a difference. At the end of one session, we had a spouse come up and say to us, "Two weeks ago I had asked for a divorce just so I could leave Germany. I just couldn't survive here. Now I know I can. I have friends, I know my child is okay in daycare, I have activities I'm interested in—and I even know how to use the bus to go downtown and order items in stores." Talk about a sense of satisfaction!

The irony is that after two years, I was hired to do the program for pay as a contractor, something I hadn't even envisioned. The greater irony is that in 1996 we returned to Bamberg where I had my twins and ended up being a single mom and head of our Family Readiness Group when my husband's unit deployed for ten months. I would not have survived that deployment and time as well as I did without that deep knowledge of Bamberg, the military community, and its resources. I would not have had that knowledge without my involvement with PEP.

Look around your military community. So many of the programs that help to make this challenging life easier or richer came about because someone—often another military spouse—saw a need and set out to fill that need. Because of volunteers, we have programs such as Army (and Marine Corps) Family Team Building, marine's L.I.N.K.S., Navy COMPASS, and Air Force Heart Link. We also have children's sports programs and other youth enrichment programs such as the School of the Arts in Heidelberg. Specifically for spouses there are new spouse orientation programs and the amazing spouse conferences held in Germany, Hawaii, Fort Lewis, Fort Benning, and other places. There are also many important programs outside our military installations that can use our help. It's another way to connect to local communities.

Volunteering Increases Your Energy and Happiness

When you are truly generous without thought of gaining something back in return, you get a warm, fuzzy feeling inside—an actual biochemical response—that has been called a "helper's high." Not only do you make a difference in someone else's life by your volunteer efforts, you make a difference in your own. Volunteering increases your psychological and physical well being. It can even add a few extra years to your life, according to research at both Cornell University and the University of Michigan. The Cornell Study showed that actively involved women have high self-esteem, enjoy greater total well being, and are more likely to live longer than those women who aren't involved. The Michigan study showed that people live longer because they volunteer, rather than that people volunteer because they're healthier and hence likely to live longer.

Volunteering can increase your energy. When Holly co-created the PEP orientation program in Bamberg, Germany, she worked well over forty hours a week. She was full of energy and enthusiasm and excited to get going every day. That's what happens when you volunteer for a project that you are excited about. When you do something challenging that you care deeply about, you can easily lose sense of time. You are in flow, which is one of the times that cause true happiness in life.

Volunteering can also help combat depression. According to Richard O'Connor, Ph.D., psychologist and author of *Undoing Depression,* one way to pull yourself out of depression is to connect with others. Doing a good deed for others is particularly powerful, he adds. By volunteering you do both. You connect with others and do good deeds.

As army spouse, Natalie Finley, wrote in a letter to the *Army Times* newspaper in response to another spouse's letter titled "Alone at Home," "I encourage all you lonely spouses out there to get involved. Loneliness is a choice you make by doing nothing. Once you get involved and meet people, your life will be richer for it, and the time during deployments will be much more bearable."

Stephanie Pompa was a Family Readiness Group (FRG) leader for Bravo Company of the Twenty-ninth Signal Battalion, a Fort Lewis unit deployed to Iraq. When SFC Tommy Carson wrote the FRG asking for Tootsie Pops for soldiers to give out to Iraqi children, Stephanie enlisted other spouses to collect more than two hundred fifty bags of Tootsie Pops. When the battalion adopted a school, Carson wrote about how little the children have. "He said they don't have shoes so their feet were cut up and bleeding," says Stephanie. Her group of spouses collected four-hundred backpacks with school supplies and more than three hundred pairs of shoes by calling on churches, schools, businesses, Girl Scout troops, and getting local media coverage. The soldiers built a new school and the spouses provided school supplies. "Volunteering was one of the ways I made it through that deployment," says Stephanie. "My time spent working on that project every day made those first six months fly by. It made me feel good to feel I was making a difference."

Susan Agustin, an army spouse, discovered Huggee Miss You dolls when relatives sent one to her three-year-old daughter Maddie with photos of her cousins to keep in front of her. These simple cloth stuffed dolls have a plastic sleeve instead of a face, a spot to place the photo of a loved one. "When my husband Gene deployed to Qatar, daddy's photo replaced the cousins," says Susan. The "Daddy Doll" went everywhere with Maddie. In fact, Gene would call and ask, "Where did we go and what did we do today?" The teachers at her daughter's school told her that every child dealing with deployments or any parental absence needs one of those dolls. Susan finally started selling them on post and through a website. She also created a way to allow Family Support Groups and other military spouse groups to sell the dolls as fundraisers.

Susan realized quickly that a business wasn't what she was about. "I just wanted to get these dolls into the hands of children who needed them—the over 200,000 children affected by deployment," she says. She chose to close her business and start a volunteer program called Operation Give a Hug (www.operationgiveahug.org) where she collected donations from businesses to get these dolls into the hands of as many children of deployed military as possible. "If you'd ever told me I'd be speaking in front of large groups of business people," she adds, "I wouldn't have believed you. But when you are passionate about something, you step outside your comfort zone."

Susan and Stephanie's stories are just a few of many. The military has always run on volunteerism, with military members and family members making a difference on post/base and off, and in foreign lands. They end up making a difference to themselves too. Research shows that giving altruistically is one key way to experience lasting happiness. It turns out that making a difference is contagious as well.

Research by Jonathan Haidt, Ph.D., an associate professor of psychology at the University of Virginia, suggests that seeing or even reading about others' generosity can not only make us better people, but increases the likelihood we'll do good works of our own. What he terms "elevation" is what happens when we witness acts of moral beauty (e.g., compassion, courage, loyalty, generosity). Elevation elicits a physical sensation of warmth or openness in the chest and motivates people to help others or to become better people themselves. As Haidt says, "Recognize that your own actions often have a ripple effect that you don't realize."

Volunteering really is a win/win situation. You can fill a need in the community. You can increase your own happiness and sense of satisfaction in life. You can connect more deeply to the community you live in. You might even trigger generosity in others around you. And you can learn skills that you want to learn.

Volunteering Develops Skills

Janet Farley, author of *Jobs and the Military Spouse* and the *Military-to-Civilian Career Transition Guide*, credits her volunteer work with Army Community

Service for getting her the job as a Career Counselor with Resource Consult-ants, Inc. (RCI). "The job required actual teaching experience," she says. "They accepted my Army Community Service training experience in lieu of paid teach-ing experience." The job with RCI eventually led her to write her books.

You can build the skills you need through volunteer opportunities. Kathie did that with writing and speaking and desktop publishing. Nada and Holly did that with learning about the military and their communities and sharing that knowledge with other spouses.

Listen to how marine spouse Lori Cleymans describes her experience. "I am currently a career counselor at Camp Pendleton. What I find with many military spouses is they don't have the skills to compete in today's workforce or they lack direction in their career search. I was one of them when I first married my marine. I assumed my degree would guarantee me work. However, when I went on job interviews, they didn't ask about my degree; they asked about my skills and experience, what I had to offer. Having been only a full-time student, I had no skills except how to study.

"After six months of job searching, I was still unemployed, bored out of my mind, and clinging to my husband because he was the only person I could talk to. I finally started volunteering out of desperation. From working at the thrift shop to acting as Key Volunteer Coordinator for my husband's unit to becoming publicity chair for L.I.N.K.S. and other programs, I started develop-ing skills. With our move to Okinawa, I volunteered as publicity chair for Navy/ Marine Corps Relief Society, continuing to hone my public speaking skills and building my resume.

"When I started job interviews again, I had skills to sell. I got the first job I tried for as outreach coordinator for the University of Maryland. With my next move, I once again got the first job I applied for now that my two-page resume is filled with skills and experience (the bulk of it gained in volunteerism).

"Through volunteering, I gained experience and skills, I've met lots of great people who helped me grow, and I've discovered who I am."

Not only can you develop career skills, you develop life skills. We've watched people blossom through volunteering. One extremely shy friend started volunteering with Army Family Team Building, went through the Train the Trainer program, and ended up as a master trainer. You should see her now— poised, self-confident, well spoken.

Volunteering often pays back later in ways you don't anticipate—in new passions or career paths—in contacts that bring you jobs or friends later—in skills that are exactly what you need down the road for another important project or for your business or career.

What's hard to document but easy to see with the people around you is the level of personal growth that can develop from volunteer projects you are passionate about. Only *you* can truly prove to yourself the level of satisfaction and joy that comes from it.

Be Aware! Volunteering Can Also Cause Problems

You know the saying, "You can have too much of a good thing." Well, it applies to volunteering too. Just because there is a need to be filled, doesn't always mean that you are the best person to fill it at this time. You've also heard, "If you want something done, give it to the busy person." Well, that may be true, but only to a point. Sometimes that person becomes too busy because she just don't know how to say no to requests.

We have both been in situations ourselves and watched many friends get into the situations of committing to too much. The result can include extreme stress or even illness for the individual, and neglect of her family. It can mean that an important volunteer task doesn't get done as effectively as it might. That does not fit into the win/win formula of healthy volunteerism.

It's important to make conscious choices in volunteering just as it is important to do so in the rest of your life. Those choices should be made based on a number of factors—the importance of the task, your own family priorities and schedules, your interest in the project, and possibly the opportunity to learn something new that you want to learn.

Vivian Rhodes, a very active volunteer and highly esteemed army spouse, offered Holly countless tips and tools for dealing with the challenges of military life. Vivian always encouraged Holly to take care of herself, her children, and her husband first before thinking of delving into a new volunteer project. She suggests that you delegate what you can, and if no one else wants to do it, then let it go. You might have to ask yourself, "What does it really matter in the light of eternity?"

When faced with a decision to volunteer for something or not, Vivian recommends asking yourself the simple question, "What part of this activity will energize me?" If you are energized by the thought of getting involved, then say yes. If just the thought of it drains and depresses you, then don't do it. Trust your gut. If it energizes you, go for it. If you don't have the emotional, physical, or spiritual energy for the task, don't take it on.

We've both been in the position of asking for volunteers. We don't want someone to do a task begrudgingly with a bad attitude—or simply not enough time or energy—just because they weren't able to say no to us when we asked them to do it. The last thing we would want is to cause someone family or health problems because of time spent volunteering for our project.

Saying no can take practice. We saw a button once that said, "Stress is what happens when your gut says no and your mouth says 'Sure, I'd be glad to.'" Give yourself time to listen to your gut. One good first step is to give yourself space to make a conscious decision by saying, "Let me check my calendar and get back with you."

And by the way, often the problem isn't that you want to say no, it's that the reality of your current life situation is that you need to say no. Here are some good questions to ask yourself when you are asked to do something you'd like to say yes to, but that you know will make your life crazy if you do say yes.

- Is it necessary? Does it fit in with my values and priorities?
- Will this opportunity come around again?
- Can I shift something else or delegate something to make space?
- Can I cut anything else out?
- If none of those are possible, are my family and I willing to take on a time period of craziness in order to say yes to this? If so, *no* whining allowed!

It's important that we all learn to say no graciously when no is the right answer for us at the time. It's important that we role model that healthy practice for other military spouses and for our kids.

It's also important that we are clear that a volunteer task is a necessary and useful task, whether we are asking someone else to take it on or if we are taking it on ourselves. We can probably all share examples of things we've been asked to do that didn't make sense and didn't serve a real purpose. In some cases, the tasks were a result of outdated practices and "the way we've always done it" thinking. It's up to all of us to work toward useful, meaningful, and conscious volunteering. We really can make it win/win by making conscious choices.

Volunteering can change your life and connect you with an amazing community. As army spouse Theresa Donahoe says, "Volunteering gives me a group of people outside my home and my neighborhood to fill my mind and perhaps become my newest 'family' in the absence of my own."

Action Steps

Take the Color Test

Kathie's Story

Many years ago, feeling overwhelmed, stressed out, and not really happy with my life, I stumbled on a book with a title that fit my mood: Women and the Blues, *by Jennifer James. It's full of great ideas and exercises, but one exercise stands out in my memory because it had a huge impact on me. I call it the color test.*

Using three different colored highlighters, you mark up your cal-endar pages from the last quarter. I used my favorite color blue to mark those activities that I did that were things I wanted to do that worked me toward my dreams. In yellow, I marked all those activities that were maintenance type things, things that just plain have to be done in life whether I enjoy them or not. I chose pink (not my favorite color) to highlight all those activities that I did not enjoy, that did not work toward my dreams, and that were items I could have said "no" to. My calendar was covered in pink and yellow with very little blue.

Okay, I already knew that, but seeing it in black and white—I mean, in color—shocked me into action. I had to learn how to say no to the things I didn't want to do so that I would have time to say yes to the things I do want to do. I had to make conscious choices about my time and energy.

Do your own color test. It might just help you say no the next time you get asked to take on a project that doesn't fit in with your priorities and your family's priorities.

What Skill Do You Want to Use or Learn?

Where could you apply that skill? What volunteer organization or project holds meaning for you *and* gives you the chance to learn or improve a skill that is important to you?

Resources

Undoing Depression, by Richard O'Connor, PhD [1999].

How to Say No Without Feeling Guilty...and say YES to more time, more joy, and what matters most to you by Patti Breitman and Connie Hatch(2000).

Women and the Blues: Passions That Hurt, Passions That Heal by Jennifer James (1990).

Interested in volunteering on base/post? The Volunteer Coordinator at your family service center will know what all is available at that location and can help you find the best fit for you.

Chapter 11

Try These Effective and Fun Goal Achieving Techniques

How to Move Toward Your Goals Even as You Move with the Military

Whatever your dreams and goals are—whether personal, family, community, career, business, or education—let's look at ways to take action to achieve them.

Choose a Primary Focus for Each Stage of Life

Before we get into the how-to of achieving your goals, there is a key concept to consider—the concept of Primary Focus.

Kerry Vosler is a portrait artist who takes her art business seriously. She's also a mom and military spouse. She knew the upcoming deployment of her husband's unit would take up all of her time. As the brigade commander's wife with two children at home, her art business would have to step back during that time period. To prepare for that circumstance, she took a few months ahead of that time to focus almost exclusively on her art. As soon as her husband and kids were out of the house each morning, she put a sign on her door that read, "Working on a project, please come back later," turned the music on, and painted with abandon until her youngest son got home from school.

When the deployment happened and her life was consumed with acting as a single parent and helping the other families, she didn't resent the disruption. She had prepared for it by taking the time for her art first. She chose one primary focus for each of those times, rather than drive herself crazy trying to do everything at once.

When you dream *big,* you will most likely find that you will come up with some goals that seem to conflict. The truth is that if you try to approach every single one of your goals at the same time, you will only get frustrated.

Holly's Story

We dreamed big, set goals, and made plans for our seminars when we lived in Germany. We started speaking all over Europe, having a blast, and making a difference in other people's lives. Then something else wonderful happened. I became pregnant with twins after twelve years of trying. I needed to make a hard decision. Speaking and traveling all over the place were not conducive to the goals I had set for myself as a mother. Yet—believe it or not—I felt torn. I loved speaking and helping other military spouses—it truly feeds my soul.

A passage from the book CARE Packages for the HOME, *by Barbara Glanz, helped me at that time. "Choose a primary focus for each stage of life and be intensely committed to it! If you have decided what your PRIMARY focus is at this point in time, it will help you make hard choices a little easier. A primary focus gives you a frame for the way you approach the world. For example, if you have decided that your children are your primary focus at this point in time, then it will be easier to make decisions when you are offered a promotion in your part time job. One of the things I used in my "self talk" when I was confused and torn between a desire to be successful in my career and to stay at home with my children was to remind myself that other jobs would always be out there if I kept my skills honed, while my children would be young only once. I was merely postponing one wonderful thing for another!"*

I took Barbara's advice to heart. I chose to focus on my twins and still find small ways to keep my speaking skills alive. I created ways to speak occasionally without leaving home or leaving my kids. Because of my two master's degrees and teaching background in early childhood and special education, I found it easy to share my knowledge about child development and behavior modification in workshops for other mothers in neighborhood playgroups and church groups. I also shared with other military spouses about deployments and how to get through them.

With my primary focus clearly in mind, saying no to speaking engagements that required travel became easier. My primary focus when my children were little was to be with them. By keeping my skills honed, I was ready to start speaking again on occasion four years later. I still only travel when it can work for my family.

Do you have something you need to focus on at this point in time in your life? If so—do that. Identify what your primary focus is and be intensely committed to it. Get in there and enjoy that part of your life. Every chapter of life has some blessings to focus on. Don't push off the other dreams totally. If you fit in small bits and pieces for now, your other dreams don't die out. Remember it is not reaching that *big* dream that brings you joy in your life. It is the fact that you have identified what that dream is and you are taking steps to add it into your life in some manner. It is enjoying the process along the way—that's what brings joy into life on a daily basis.

This concept is important to keep in mind during deployments. If you have children at home, they are going to need even more of your time and energy during a deployment than at other times. At the same time, you are taking on 100 percent of the household chores. Depending on your level of support, your finances, your own organizational skills, and energy level, this may well be one time where your primary focus is spelled out clearly for you as a parent.

Apply the Basics of Effective Goal Setting and Achieving

- Identify the goal and the benefits to you. Be sure the goal is in line with your values.
- Commit to it by writing it down. Research shows that you are 25 percent more likely to achieve your goal simply by writing it down than if you just have it "in your head."
- Set a deadline. Deadlines are often what we need to get ourselves to start moving forward. They give you a checkpoint to measure your progress. (Of course, we know that things will happen in military life that will make some deadlines impossible. Don't worry; deadlines aren't carved in stone. Just set one—it gives you a reason to start moving!)
- Set a start date and schedule it in your calendar.
- Come up with a plan of action—the mini steps that will work you toward your goal.
- Take action.
- Build in accountability.
- Celebrate success!

The first step in effective goal setting is to make sure the goal is truly *your* goal. Write the goal down and then write down the benefits to you. What's in it for you? Why do you want to achieve this particular goal? How will you and your life be different by accomplishing this goal? What values does your goal support? (And if you've never taken time to clarify your values, do the values exercises on our website.)

If you have trouble identifying the benefit to you and the values that it supports, then it is probably not your goal. It's most likely someone else's goal for you. We don't know about you, but we have too many things we want to achieve in our lives to be wasting time on other people's goals for us.

By clearly identifying the benefit to you, you create a stronger magnet of a goal to pull you forward. Clear, compelling benefits can pull you around obstacles that show up in your way.

As Barbara Sher says, "What is the touchstone?" What are your own criteria for success in that goal? Or, as Dr. Phil says, "How would that make you feel? So, what you really want is to feel . . . ?" Knowing your touchstone allows you more flexibility in your goal setting, in how you actually get to the goal.

Determine the Outcome of Your Outcomes

Another way to look at the benefits/touchstone of your goal comes from Henriette Klauser, a former navy spouse, mother of four (including one daughter currently in the navy), and author of the terrific book, *Write It Down and Make It Happen*.

Henriette asks you to determine your "outcome of outcomes." "Instead of just writing your goal, consider why you want the goal in the first place, how attaining it will enrich your life or other's lives," she suggests. This takes it even deeper than that benefit to you. What will your life be like if you go for that goal?

There are so many goals that we might not be able to go for fully at the moment because of where we are located or what our life is currently like because of our military life. But there may be a way to still get at least part of the "outcome of the outcomes."

For example, Susan is a navy spouse and mother of two. One of her goals is to go for her master's of fine arts (MFA) degree in creative writing. That isn't possible right now, time-wise, location-wise, and finances-wise. But the "outcome of the outcome" for her is that she wants to immerse herself more fully in the writing world, to become a more creative writer, to build her confidence and credibility to sell more of her writing and to get books published, to eventually make a good living with her writing.

Okay, so what can she do right now—without the MFA program—to achieve that?

- Read books and magazines about the writing craft,
- Start or join a writer's group,
- Attend local writing workshops,

- Attend book readings that come to town,
- Join a professional writer's association for information and networking.

Most importantly, she can do all of that right now, right here, while she builds up her savings for the MFA for when her life situation allows for that total immersion. Who knows, she may decide later that she doesn't even need the MFA.

So, what's the "outcome of the outcomes" for your dream? What can you do right here, right now, to bring you some of that outcome? Maybe you need to look for the second, third, or higher right answer for your goals.

Brainstorm Second and Third Right Answers

In our workshops we give participants an opportunity to share dreams and brainstorm with the group for the second/third right answer.

Charmin Foth's dream was to own and run a bed and breakfast (B&B) in Tennessee. When asked at a Fort Stewart, Georgia, workshop for her plan of action, she started with, "We hope to get stationed to . . ." and "as soon as he retires, I'll . . . " Notice how those are actions outside of her own control and focused on future events. When we pushed for things she could do now, she added a few: read books on running B&B's, search the Internet for information, collect breakfast recipes.

We then asked the other workshop attendees for help. Ideas flew.

- Join the B&B association for information and contacts,
- Intern at a B&B to learn the ropes, or "baby-sit" one while the owners take a vacation,
- Take a class locally on how to run a small business—taxes, accounting, marketing, and so on.

By the time we finished brainstorming, her eyes were shining as she saw possibilities. Imagine the fun and excitement that Charmin can now create in her life right away and anywhere they are stationed—moving toward her dream.

The key is realizing there are paths you can try out, rather than simply seeing a dead end in front of you. Brainstorming with others is the first open gate on the road to possibilities.

It's simply a reality of military life. Some things you want to do aren't possible, at least not exactly the way you envision them. Your career won't proceed in a straight-line fashion. You can't build your business the same effective, consistent way your peers who stay put can. You won't have that dream house you keep working on year in and year out to get it just the way you want. You won't have a garden that matures and evolves over time.

Many of your dreams may seem impossible where you happen to be assigned at the moment. Does that mean you have to give your dream up? No. It just means the approach you are thinking of—your first right answer—won't work right here.

That's where second/third and higher "right answers" come into play.

The key is realizing there are paths you can try out, rather than simply seeing a dead end in front of you. If your first right answer isn't possible, look for the second right answer, or as many as you need until you find one that will work right now, right where you are. This is such an important concept to get.

Too many of us stop with the first solution to our situation. If that solution isn't possible, we often just give up and end up frustrated and angry with the military—for moving us in the first place or for sticking us in this "godforsaken place." (We know from experience since we each did that in early assignments.)

By looking for, and finding, the right answer that does work right where you are, you keep moving toward your dream. You can be quite content wherever they send you as you take advantage of the possibilities of each new assignment.

Let's look at some more examples of how this works:

Janie, a navy spouse, worked as a secretary for many years and had been able to move that career as she moved with the military. Then she moved with her husband to a small military community in Japan. There were no secretarial jobs at her level and in fact there weren't any secretarial jobs open at the time.

Janie could have stopped there, frustrated and angry for three years. Instead she decided to look at the situation differently. "Although I've always worked as a secretary because I'm good at it and the pay was good," she says, "my dream has always been to open a bakery." She decided to see this move as a forced golden opportunity to move toward her dream. She took a job at a submarine sandwich shop operating off base.

"I couldn't have justified doing that in the States where the secretarial pay is so much higher than the minimum wage I earn here," she says. "I don't see myself as a minimum wage worker at a sub shop, however. I see myself as getting paid to take a hands-on course in small business management." She learned everything she could about the ins and outs of a small business, in preparation for her own future business. Now that's a second right answer!

Diana McCarthy is an army spouse who wanted to go to law school, but that wasn't available where they were living in Germany. She figured she'd have to wait until they returned to the United States and just hoped to be stationed near a law school. When she shared that dream and first right answer with our workshop group, the ideas flew.

We received this email from her a few weeks later. "I just wanted to let you know you have motivated and made a difference in my life. I have volunteered for the local JAG office and signed up for distance learning law classes as I go to the library and check out books all the time to help me with my law career." She paid attention to the second and third right answers that came out of the brainstorming session and took action to start moving toward her dream—without any change of assignment or circumstances.

Phyllis Ward is an army spouse who worked as a sports/fitness specialist in Germany at the post fitness center. When they moved to Colorado Springs she was unable to get back into the GS system in that field. At first she accepted a bookkeeping position, but soon tired of sitting at a desk. She decided to take a leap of faith and start her own personal training business to put her fitness experience back to work. She quit her job and within twenty-four hours had seven clients. "My fitness experience with the military is impressive to people—it helps in my marketing."

Kathie's Story

I started doing seminars when my husband was assigned to Fort Lewis, Washington. I landed an audition with one of the national seminar companies to possibly do programs for them all over the United States. My new business was on its way!

Then we got orders to Germany. The national seminar company unfortunately had no work for me overseas. In order to market my seminars to corporations in Germany, I would have to pay German taxes. My business wasn't large enough or advanced enough to justify that. I thought I'd have to give up seminar work for three years. My first right answer just wasn't possible in Germany.

At a newcomer welcome luncheon I happened to talk with a spouse who told me about the American Women's Activities Germany conference held every year. The proposals for workshops were due that week. Talk about serendipity. Another new acquaintance told me about the Office of Personnel Management—how they provide training workshops to offices all through Europe. Their headquarters happened to be a two-hour drive from where we lived.

I spent the next three years doing all kinds of seminars for military spouse groups and for military offices throughout Europe. I was able to build my skills, material, and reputation, and continue in this field I had almost given up on during that assignment. and I was now able to market myself as an "international speaker," something it might have taken me years longer to achieve living in the United States. Not to mention the fact that I got to travel to wonderful places like Garmisch, Germany, and Venice, Italy, to speak. And it all happened because other spouses opened me up to second and third right answers to what I wanted to do.

One thing we want to mention. At one of our workshops, as we described the concept of second "right" answers, a military spouse challenged us. "That still sounds like you are making a sacrifice, since you can't go after what you want the way you want," she said. Well, that is one way to look at it. And yes, the reality is that we are making sacrifices as military spouses—just as our spouses are making sacrifices by serving in the military. There is no question that life might be much easier and more straightforward if we weren't married to the military. But the fact remains that we are.

So, from there, choosing to look for the second, third, and higher right answer simply makes sense. Your other option is to simply give up when the first way doesn't work and to wallow in frustration and bitterness. Instead, doesn't it make sense to be creative, and to get the help of other creative people to find an answer that does work? The interesting thing is, often that second, third, or higher right answer ends up being a better route in the long run anyway. The most important thing is that it keeps you making forward progress and not giving up on your dream. Sacrifice or innovation? Whatever it is, it keeps you moving toward your dreams!

And remember, the research shows that it isn't achieving your goal that brings you joy—it's the fact that you've identified your goal or dream and you are working toward it in some manner. That's what brings the joy!

Develop a Plan of Action and Get Moving

Okay, so you know what you want to take action on even here where you are stationed. How do you move forward?

First, come up with a plan of action. Here's one great way to do so. Start by using a blank sheet of paper. Put your goal in the center of it. First, write the benefits to you in the upper left corner. Then simply brainstorm with yourself.

Think of all the things you could do that can move you toward the goal. Think of the people and organizations you need to work with, the skills you need, the resources you need to tap into. Write them all over that page. Don't worry about order or priority right now. You can even draw pictures of what you need. Adding color and sketches activates your creative right brain.

Then set it aside for a few days or a week. That gives your subconscious a chance to work on this. Come back to it with a fresh mind to see what you can add. Now you can take the time to prioritize the steps, to break big steps into smaller steps, and to schedule these smaller steps into your calendar.

To make this even more effective, once you have the basic brainstorm down, gather a group of friends. Four to six is good. Put what you've come up with on a big piece of flip chart paper on the wall. Tell them what your goal is and ask if they have any other ideas, contacts, or resources to add to your plan of action. The ideas will fly, synergy will step in, and you'll come up with a much more complete plan of action.

As an added bonus, you now have all these other folks who know your dream and will help you along—with ideas, with resources and contacts, and with a bit of accountability as they ask you how you are doing. (Why would they do this for you? Hey, they are your friends! Plus, once they see the power of this you can return the favor and do the same for them.)

Remember—we can't emphasize this enough! The research shows that it isn't achieving the goal that brings the joy; it's the process of working toward the goal, the fact that you are moving toward what you want. Don't agonize over the plan of action itself. Just come up with one and start moving forward. Your plan will change as you are out there discovering new things. (Plus, neurology researchers have found that diving into a new experience triggers the production of dopamine, one of the body's feel-good chemicals, so you'll immediately up your happiness by taking on the new.)

One great way to get you moving forward is to schedule appointments with yourself in your calendar or day planner, in ink, to work toward your goal, to take the mini steps one at a time.

Once you make a commitment and start moving forward, things will happen that you could never have planned on. You may find you reach your goal in a completely different way than you could ever have expected. But it will happen because you are out trying to make things happen. It won't happen if you just sit at home and watch TV or complain about your situation.

Open Yourself Up to Serendipity

Kerry Vosler, army spouse and artist, does not have an art degree. "I pieced my career together over time as we moved, by working with artists one-on-one, by going to workshops, by self study and doing art," she says. She has taught art in schools and one-on-one out of her home. She has created many portraits on commission.

At one point, when they had just moved to Missouri, she got discouraged. "It was pretty dry for artists," she explains. She volunteered some time with a Chautauqua conference there, creating their advertising poster. A contact from that organization led her to an interview with and a commission to do the portrait of Ike Skelton.

"Just when I thought my art career was over," she says, "I got asked to do a portrait of the leading Democrat at the time." That has led to more work. That is serendipity. (You'll notice she wasn't sitting at home doing nothing but bemoaning her fate when the opportunity came up. She was actively out in the community, moving forward, doing something with her art, even when it seemed like limited forward movement.)

We've experienced serendipity ourselves many times over. We had been volunteering our seminars for military spouses all over Germany for three years. Newly returned to the states, we heard they were sending soldiers to Bosnia for a year—the longest deployment for the army at that time since Vietnam. We thought, "We want to do seminars for those spouses." But we didn't think the army would pay to bring us back to Germany, so we brainstormed different ways to make it happen.

We decided we would have to get a corporate sponsor. To create the best proposal possible, we figured we had better get some testimonials from spouses who had participated in our workshop. We sent out letters to them. All of a sudden, we got an email from the spouse of the army's commander in chief of troops in Europe (CINCUSAREUR) saying our letter had been passed on to her from one of the women we sent it to. They had just been discussing the need for something like this. There were family support funds available. The seminars happened—not the way our goal plan said—but serendipitously in a quicker way, because we'd been taking action and moving forward.

The key is that you aren't sitting back just waiting for something to happen, just waiting for someone else to step in, just waiting for the perfect assignment or circumstance. That would be like the Chinese proverb: "A peasant must stand a long time on a hillside with his mouth open before a roast duck flies in." You need to be out there taking steps, starting the momentum. And then, things happen! Who knows? That roast duck might even show up.

As Oprah says: "The truth is that as much as you plan and dream and move forward in your life, you want to remember you are always acting in conjunction with the flow and energy of the universe. You move in the direction of your goal with all the force and verve you can muster—and then let go, releasing your plan to the power that's bigger than yourself and allow your dream to unfold as its own masterpiece."

Set Short-Term and Long-Term Goals, Big and Small

Kerry, the artist, suggests you set a really long-term high level "in the clouds" goal. Her long-term goal is to become known as an American master painter, recognized by her peers and the country.

We've heard these bigger goals described as BHAGs—Big Hairy Audacious Goals! Doesn't that make it sound like more fun? But as Kerry adds, "Set some flexible realistic short term goals for yourself as well." With this military life, you will face challenges and you won't be able to follow a straight-line path forward. By having some smaller goals that you can achieve more quickly, you see success. Once you see success in one goal, you'll be encouraged to go for your next one.

As Kerry says, "The reality of this military lifestyle is that you have to keep your expectations in check a bit, otherwise you can feel like a failure." That is especially true if you constantly compare your level of success in whatever you do with your peers who are not moving every three years, who are not dealing with deployments and other military challenges. "For me," Kerry says, "as long as I continue to see progress, I feel successful."

> "Success occurs when you chase the dream and not the competition."
> —*Unknown*

Remember what the happiness research shows. The joy is in the journey, in the fact that you are doing something for you that you are interested in, that you are engaged in life. You aren't always putting your needs and interests on the back burner waiting for retirement or some other distant future. Write down your big goals, but start by working toward one smaller short-term goal. Make it a little bigger than what you think is realistic, so that you have to stretch yourself a bit.

Create a Visual Treasure Map of Your Dreams

Kathie first learned about this tool from her friend Reba who had created photo books of her dreams. Reba had some pretty amazing, almost magical results. For one example, she was single but wanted to be in a relationship. She found photos of couples who looked like they were in love, mostly sitting on beaches and at island resorts and added those to her book. Reba would look at her photo book every night before she went to sleep and each morning when she first got up. A few years later, she met her husband—at a conference on an island!

Dixie Schneider wanted to speak on cruise ships. She's a bit zany, so she used a different variation of treasure maps. She got cruise ship brochures from a travel agency, cut out the photos and put them all over her house. Open the refrigerator and there would be a photo of a cruise ship. Open the medicine cabinet door and there would be a cruise ship. Lift the toilet seat and there would be a cruise ship. Her air force engineer husband gave her a lot of grief, as you can imagine.

Well, Dixie has spoken on cruise ships all over the world. The first opportunity came by sheer serendipity. A former speech instructor of hers ran into her at the grocery store. He said, "I hear you are doing motivational speaking now. I was scheduled to speak on an upcoming cruise, but my mother is ill and I can't do the cruise. Could you take my place?" Could she?!

Now did those things happen by magic just because of the photos? No, of course not. Reba didn't just sit at home looking yearningly at the photo book. She was actively involved in interesting things, taking classes, taking action that happened to put her on the right island at the right time. Dixie didn't just look at the cruise ship photos and wait. She took steps, studying and learning how to be a speaker, doing free and then paid speaking, developing her platform and business skills, gaining visibility and a good reputation. She scoured thrift shops to buy evening gowns and cruise type outfits so she'd be ready. When the first opportunity to speak on a cruise ship appeared, she was ready to take advantage of the opportunity. And she did a great job so she continued to get asked back.

What happens with treasure mapping is that by keeping the images of what you want clearly in front of you, you do not let yourself forget. You are pulled toward your dreams. Because the goal is so vivid in your mind, you start making choices, you start taking action, and you start taking steps that move you toward that dream. (Okay, we admit, we think there is a little bit of magic involved as well! The universe seems to step in to help.)

You can do this by yourself or gather a group of friends for a fun night. You know all those magazines you've been meaning to read, those piles that add to your clutter guilt? Put them to good use and clear them out at the same time. Buy some poster board or foam core (this is thicker and lasts longer as you move these in your military moves). We've found that black makes a more dramatic backing to the photos than white does. Put on fun music. Cut out photos of your dreams. Cut out headlines or make your own on the computer (with large type) and cut those out to fit. Put a photo of yourself in the center of the board and then surround yourself with your dreams. Show your friends and describe what each visual means to you. Hang this in a place where you will see it every day . . . and watch the magic happen.

Encourage your children to make their own treasure maps. You can even make a family one. One of our friends created a 3-D one. Another family each makes a placemat-size treasure map each year. They laminate them and use them at meals during the year so they keep their goals right in front of them on a daily basis.

Kathie's Story

I started out with a photo book too. I think I was a little self-conscious about my dreams. They seemed a bit lofty and impossible for someone like me. Who was I to think I could do these things? I wasn't quite ready to have them out in the open for comments from my husband and anyone who came in my house. So I used the book and kept it to myself at first.

I included photos of myself with headlines cut from magazines—Successful Speaker, Successfully Published Author. This was all before I ever started my writing and right as I had just done my very first free seminar at McChord AFB. I included photos of material things I wanted, like a massage table (some day I want regular massages at home!), a hot tub, and a sauna (I come from a long line of Finns who had these in their homes). I included photos of women who looked confident and elegant and included the headlines: Confidence, Energy, Simply Elegant. I had a photo of a beautiful garden and the headline: A Life-Long Garden, Flowers All Year Long.

I now proudly hang treasure maps around my house, mostly in my home office where I spend much of my time. Six years after I did my first poster Treasure Map, I started a support group in Corvallis, Oregon. I suggested to them that we make treasure maps and showed them mine. My new friend Claire said, "I don't get it. This IS your life. These are mostly photos of what you already have. How does that move you forward?" She was right. Almost everything in that first treasure map had already happened in some way. That's the magic.

"That's just it," I told her, "I had none of those things in my life back when I put this together in 1990. It did draw me forward and now I want to make a new one for future possibilities."

A side note about the "magic" of this. As we started editing this book, I dug up my first photo book treasure map that I hadn't looked at in many years. I called Holly excitedly. "You won't believe this!" One photo I had was of a sailboat leaving a harbor in the Virgin Islands, with my headline "Sailing in the Virgin Islands," not something we'd taken any action on since we saw that as a retirement dream. Well, this past year, our neighbors' daughter asked us if we'd fill in for a couple that couldn't join them in a long-planned sailing trip. We had enough frequent flyer miles to get there for free and the trip itself was very inexpensive (with 8 of us on a 6-person boat). Here's the magic— we had done nothing to make this happen except be good neighbors. And by chance we sailed out of the exact small harbor that was in the photo in my treasure book! Now that's magic!

Get Your Spouse's Support

Heidi Rafferty is an army spouse who is pursuing a freelance writing business. To get started, she sent a lot of letters to editors and directed them to her website for further samples. "My husband helped me get all the letters out and he created the website," she adds.

Kerry, the artist, tells us "Whenever I went to a workshop, my husband supported that—he took care of our two kids."

Monica Dixon is an army spouse with two boys. She managed to get her doctorate despite many moves and one unaccompanied tour. Her research on body image and women's sexuality resulted in speaking engagements, a television interview, and a book deal. "In order to write the book," she says, "I had to physically leave home every three to four months for a weeklong period. My husband took care of the children, and an amazing thing happened—he became a dad!" She couldn't have written the book without her

Just as we make adjustments and compromises to support their military work, they do the same for us, for this work we love.

husband's help. We could not do the work that we do without the support and encouragement of our husbands. Just as we make adjustments and compromises to support their military work, they do the same for us, for this work we love. Plus they are our biggest cheerleaders.

Everyone we interviewed who was involved in interests of their own mentioned the support of their spouse. Their spouse supported their interests just as they supported their spouse's military career. It's a partnership—a win/win situation.

Financing Your Dream

One important step in goal achieving, no matter what your dream, is to take control of your finances.

If we had our lives to do over, that is one big thing we'd do first. As Kathie admits, "If I were a young wife new to the military now, I know I could do a whole lot more for our family's long term financial situation if I spent some of my time learning about finances and investments rather than spending the kind of extreme time I used to spend on running or job-hunting or watching television or shopping for the best curtains for our house with each move." From what we are learning by reading about finances today, we both wish we had started much sooner. Just take a look at compound interest tables and you'll see how much better off you will be by doing even small-level investments early in life!

- Learn about the military's Thrift Savings Plan and max it out as much as possible.
- Take advantage of the financial planning workshops that are offered on military posts, and off.
- Read *Military Money* magazine. This is a publication produced in partnership between the National Military Family Association and nonprofit In Charge Publications and available free to military members and their families.
- Join an investment club to help you learn or start a Money Club (see resources). The sooner you start, the bigger impact you can have on your finances overall—and the sooner you'll have the finances to fund many of your family's dreams.

Reap the Rewards of Risk Taking

As you move toward your dreams, you end up stepping outside your comfort zone. "A ship in a harbor is safe, but that's not what ships are built for" is a quote that has helped Holly many times over the years when she was scared to take a risk. Yes, there are times when it seems a lot easier to just stay doing the same thing, but sometimes you have to get out of the harbor (your comfort zone) and set sail. You've heard the old saying, "If you always do what you've always done, you'll always get what you've always got." If you want things to change, you have to change and that often means doing something scary. As Kerry Vosler, the artist, said, "I never turned down a commission even when they were scary as hell!"

Kathie's Story
I did it! Faced a big fear and lived through it. You really do have to push through your fears if you want to grow and stretch and become more in life. It's a good idea to step outside your comfort zone every

now and then. Of course, that's easier said than done—especially if you are like me and have that tendency to be able to visualize the worst possible outcome. I'm such a worrier and I have to work hard to turn those negative pictures around and visualize positive outcomes. But I am learning to do it.

I've found it helps me to write down the expected positive outcome in my calendar for the day. So on November 22, I wrote down: "Enjoy successful radio show. Have fun!" For good measure, I added a Fantastic sticker to it.

As we were driving to AFN in Frankfurt, I told Karen that this was going to be fun. (I don't think she believed me. I don't think I believed it either.) Karen is another military spouse who I convinced to join me in this scary enterprise—a three-hour call-in radio show about careers. Neither of us had ever been on the radio and here we were committed to three hours! The listening audience would include people we live and work around, including our spouses!

In thinking back over the ways I've forced myself to face fears in the past, I realize I use a trick. Whether it was giving a seminar, doing my first keynote, going on a four-day hike, trying out rock climbing and rappelling, tackling the Team Tower, trying whitewater kayaking, or doing this radio show—in each case, I scheduled it way in advance.

Somehow, the fear isn't that big when it is so far away. And when you have so many other things going on, you sort of forget about this fear until the time comes. Where I probably wouldn't be able to say yes to something fearful if it was happening tomorrow, somehow it doesn't seem real when it is a long way off.

The other thing that helps me is reminding myself of all of those fears that are no longer fears. Certainly, in some cases, the activities I tackled, like whitewater kayaking and rock climbing, might be things that go into the "once is enough" category for me. But I'm glad I had the experience. It did increase my self-confidence. The ones I remind myself of most when facing a new fear are those that are no longer fears. I remind myself that I now really enjoy doing seminars and I loved the Hut-to-Hut hike even with a 20-lb. pack on my back.

And, yes, I really did have fun doing the call-in talk show. As Karen said afterwards, "The last thing I thought this would be was fun, but it really was!"

Tricks to Help You Take Risks:

- Tell everyone you know that you are going to do something. As one person told us, "That way there is no backing out. You have to go through with it to save face." And many friends won't let you forget. When navy spouse Sarah kept saying she wanted to try inline skating, for example, her mother and sister called her on it and bought her inline skates for her birthday. When they sat in Sarah's closet for five months, her sister came and made her try them out.

- One possible exception to the "Tell everyone you know" technique is to not tell the naysayers in your life. Instead tell positive, supportive people who will encourage you to take action. We say that because we both have enough self-doubt to start with that a naysayer just fuels our doubts and keeps us from taking action. However, we've had other spouses tell us that if someone says, "you can't do that" they then dive into action to prove that person wrong. So know yourself—if you have self-doubts avoid naysayers. If naysayers motivate you, then seek them out!

- Take someone along. It's easier to do something challenging when you do it with a friend. Our friend Jan was afraid of getting a mammogram, so she took a friend. The nurse thought it was such a great idea she said we should have a "Take Your Friend for a Mammogram Day."

- Be courageous and make mistakes. If we don't make mistakes, how do we ever learn? As Sophia Loren says, "Making mistakes is part of the dues one pays for a full life." Success doesn't come from making the fewest mistakes—it comes from getting results. You can't get results without first taking action.

- Accept that not every risk will turn into what you thought it might, but every risk you overcome will help you grow. Your courage muscle grows each time you stretch outside your comfort zone, which means you have a little more courage and confidence to take on that next risk.

- Flex your risk-taking muscle with small things. Look for daily opportunities to flex that muscle. Order a new food on a menu; take a different route to work; talk to a stranger; listen to a new kind of music. With each risk, you build your ability to take on larger ones. You expand your world experience and get out of your rut at the same time!

In the book, *Prince Charming Isn't Coming,* written by Barbara Stanny, Laura Davis says, "Through the experiences I have had and the risks I have taken, I have gained courage and confidence. I didn't start with the courage and confidence. I started with the risk."

Tara Crooks tells us how each new thing she takes on with her ArmyWifeTalkRadio.com has been very scary. She just keeps reminding herself of the scary things she's already done that worked out just fine.

We kill our fears by tackling them, by taking action. Taking action builds our self-confidence and allows us to live more fully in life.

Know That Failure Isn't Always Failure

One key thing to realize is that your goals aren't set in stone—they may very well change along the way. Sometimes what happens is that you move forward toward a goal, start to achieve it, and then realize that it isn't something you want after all.

After years of changing jobs and sometimes careers with each move, Kathie's first attempt at a business was as an Image Consultant. She spent a lot of time and money in research and setting things up, only to find out by doing that that particular business wasn't for her. Now, should she consider that a failure, a total loss? She doesn't.

"It got me into the idea of having my own business," she says. "And by doing workshops to get clients and by writing articles to get my name out there for possible clients, I learned what I really love doing." Until she started doing the workshops, she had no idea that there was any such thing as the National Speaker's Association. She now considers that first "failure" as just one important stepping stone on the path to her dreams.

We hear that from so many people as they pursue goals. Many goals lead them to other things they weren't even aware of when they got started. Plus failing at something is still better in the long run than always wondering and regretting something that you never even tried.

Monitor Your Self-Talk—The Power of Words

"Sure, I have doubts creep in," the artist Kerry admits, "but I don't listen to them—I know if you say you'll probably never be that good, you won't."

You do move in the direction that your thoughts take you. Henry Ford said, "If you think you can or you think you can't, you're right."

Note to Parents:

Holly's Story
I Can't—Yet!
We all need someone to cheer us on every now and then—especially when we get discouraged. Here's an idea to help your children build their self-esteem. Provide them with a lifetime tool on how to be their

own cheerleader when life gets them down. As mothers we need to give our children as many tools as possible to survive, because we won't always be around to pat them on the back and say, "you can do it."

Make an "I can ___" book with your children. Here's how.

Make or find any notebook (spiral is easiest). Personalize the book; make it special by decorating the cover. The title page will be "I can___." In this special book write down (or have your child write if they are old enough to write) a list of the things your child can do.

I call it an accomplishment list. It doesn't matter what age you begin. Just begin the process. You can start when your child is a baby or teenager. Record all the milestones your baby makes, like: drinks from a bottle by herself, walks by himself, poo-poos in the potty, puts his own socks on, takes turns on the swing with her friend, writes his name, puts her jacket on by herself, ties his shoes by himself. Got an A on her spelling test. Won the potato sack race at the annual picnic. Keep the list going over the years. You get the idea.

Use this special book to build your child's self esteem and to give them a tool to use when things get tough. When your child comes to you and says "but I can't do it," your first response should always be "yet . . . you can't do it . . . yet." Assure him that maybe he can't do something now, but with practice, more patience, or when he has more experience, he will be able to do it successfully.

Then if your child is still discouraged, pull out the "I can book." Review with him all the things he has been able to master, write down any new items he has been able to master, and assure him there is no doubt he will be able to master other things in the future.

We believe in the power of keeping one of these accomplishment books for ourselves as well. When we think of it we write down things we've accomplished. We include cards or notes from others when they appreciate us for something we've done. That way, when you are having a bad day, maybe feeling overwhelmed by all the things that are "yet to be done," it helps to look through these to remind yourself that you are "already quite wonderful, just the way you are." And to remind yourself that if you managed to do all of these amazing things, yes, you will learn to do that new task you've taken on. "Yes, you can!"

Think about it. You are the most powerful influence on your life. You are with yourself (and your self-talk) 24/7. The messages in your head start to become automatic and you start to believe them. "I'm always late." "I'm so tired." "I can't write." "I'm so dumb." Stop and listen to what you tell yourself. Claim the power to change those messages.

One of the most important negative messages to get out of your head is the "I can't do that because I'm married to the military" message that we were both guilty of for too many years. That constant thought keeps you from opening yourself to possibility.

When you hear yourself repeating a negative mantra, say out loud if possible, but at least loudly to yourself in your head, "Cancel!" And then switch to the positive: "Wait a minute, that's an old tape, that's not like me; that's how I used to be but I've changed." Even if you haven't yet changed, speak to yourself as if you have. You really do become what you think about most.

Kathie's Story

I was painfully shy as a child. I spent my childhood constantly reminded by teachers, peers, and family that I was the quiet one. Every report card said, "Kathie is quiet; she needs to speak up more in class." My parents said: "Kathie's the quiet one; she's the introvert; she's the bookworm." I even got voted "Most Studious" in my senior year (as you can imagine, not the title a teenage girl wants to be pegged with in high school!).

One year I decided I wanted to be more outgoing and not so painfully shy. I chose to make changes and followed up with specific actions, from running for class office to initiating conversations to eventually taking on positions in clubs I belonged to that required me to speak in front of groups. I learned the power of "Fake it 'til you make it," going into situations with positive self-talk in my head. Am I still an introvert and shy today? I am, it's my nature, but I've learned to move past that trait to get what I want in life.

For any of you with insecurities, introversion, lower self-esteem, and a history of negative self-talk, this is exactly where a support group can help. (See chapter 12 for details.)

Action Steps

Are you stuck on that first right answer for your dream? You say it's just not possible where you are living right now? Well, start looking for that second and third right answer. Enlist your friends to help brainstorm ideas. Email us. We mean it. We love to brainstorm possibilities. If we don't have ideas, we'll ask our ezine subscribers for ideas. Try us. We'd love to share your success story with others.

Resources

CARE Packages for the Home, by Barbara Glanz (1998). Kathie bought eleven of these books for friends—full of great ideas for your families. We love all of Barbara's books, including: *CARE Packages for the Workplace* and *Balancing Acts.* www.barbaraglanz.com.

Feel the Fear and Do It Anyway, by Susan Jeffers (1987).

Write It Down and Make It Happen: Knowing What You Want and Getting It, by Henriette Klauser (2000). We highly recommend all of Henriette's books, from her first, *Writing on Both Sides of the Brain* (in its 27th printing!), to her most recent, *With Pen in Hand, the Healing Power of Writing.* www.henrietteklauser.com.

Prince Charming Isn't Coming, by Barbara Stanny [1999] page 147.

Financial Resources

To understand the military pay system and learn how to read a Leave and Earnings statement, there is great information offered through programs like Army Family Team Building and the equivalent "Military 101" programs. Check with your services family support center to find out what is available. A good overview is available in Meredith Leyva's book, *Married to the Military* (2003). Chapter 7 is all about personal finances.

SaveAndInvest.org, providing tools to educate military members.

Military Money magazine. Full of good articles geared specifically to military life. Look for it in the commissary or on line at www.militarymoney.com.

How to Save Money Every Day; Money Doesn't Grow on Trees; and Shop, Save, and Share, by air force wife and mother of seven, Ellie Kay. www.elliekay.com.

Money Wi$e Women, book, forums, newsletter and resources at www.money wisewomen.net.

It's More Than Money; It's Your Life, by Candace Bahr. This book describes the Money Club concept as well. www.moneyclubs.com or www.wife.org.

The Automatic Millionaire, by David Bach, and his other books, such as *Smart Couples Finish Rich.* www.davidbach.com.

The Four Laws of Debt Free Prosperity, by Blaine Harris and Charles Coonradt with Lee Nelson (1996). A very short book in a story format that covers the basics of debt reduction, saving, and investing. A great starting point when you are short on time.

The Sailor's Savvy Spouse, by Ralph Nelson. Even though it's written for sailors (as part of a Savvy Sailor's financial book series), it's a good resource for all services. www.savvy.onweb.com.

And one great resource to get your children understanding finances at an early age is the Money Savvy Generation website (www.msgen.com). We especially love the Money Savvy Pig, a savings bank with four separate sections so your children can see their money grow for spending, saving, investing, and donating.

Chapter 12

Get Help for Your Dreams

How to Effectively Ask for and Create the Support You Need

So many of us think we have to do everything by ourselves, that we have to be totally self-motivated and self-disciplined, that we shouldn't need to ask others for any help. We've found it's much more effective and much more fun to create the support that can help you—and help others—go for your dreams. Here are some ways to do that.

Teams Help You Get What You Want

Kathie's Story
In 1989 at Fort Lewis, Washington, I decided to take a leap and start my own business—very scary! Someone heard what I was doing and said, "You should meet Reba—it sounds like you two have a lot in common." We met for a lunch that turned into one of those amazing connections. We talked non-stop for hours and came out of the restaurant full of ideas, energy, and motivation. I told Reba, "We need to keep meeting."

That is how my first support team was born. We found four other women with dreams of their own and started meeting weekly to help each other with ideas. We nudged each other along, providing the support we each needed to keep going for what we wanted. In many cases, the group first helped us figure out exactly what it was we wanted!

> *Since then, with each move, I've created a new team. Once you've been part of one, you will always want to be part of one.*
>
> *One reason groups are so important to me is that I'm a recovering procrastinator. I'm one of those people who are slow to action. I plan, research, reflect, and talk about things long before I ever act on what I want to do. I really have to trick and push myself to take action and move forward. The group helps a lot.*

So, what are these groups and why would you want to be part of one? You'll hear them called all sorts of things, from Success Teams to Mastermind groups to Boards of Directors to Life Makeover groups. We call them Dare to Dream Teams based on our current Dare to Dream column in *Military Spouse* magazine. The basic concept is the same—the group helps each member go for his or her dreams.

We could go on and on with examples of what such groups have helped people accomplish. And these are all military spouses like you. Stephanie, an army spouse wanted to learn how to work a computer. Within a few years she'd built a computer-based service company that she then sold to another firm. Army spouse Mary Styron got her resume together just because everyone else in the group was doing their resumes and she decided to tap into those resources. Within days of arriving at their next assignment, as she signed her kids up for school, she dropped off the resume to see if she could at least substitute teach. She walked out with a fulltime position.

There's more of course. Groups help you figure out how you want to live your life, what's really important to you—and they help prevent you from getting off track.

Recently we heard a woman talking about her husband deploying once again. "I gain 20 pounds every time he deploys," she said, "I guess I eat out of boredom . . . and for comfort." We immediately thought, "This woman needs a team!" Especially during deployments, your team can help you stick to good health patterns and more importantly, help you get excited about a project or goal so there's less space for the boredom and anxiety that can lead to overeating.

These groups work so well for a number of reasons.

- The accountability factor is key. You report at each meeting whether or not you accomplished the mini-goals you set the meeting before—which everyone wrote down! It's easier to justify procrastination when you are only accountable to yourself. It is much harder to face four or five other people and say, "I didn't do it—again!"

- The group expands your resources, contacts, and ideas. You are only one person with one set of experiences and ideas. Your group not only brings in all of their ideas to add to yours, but the synergy of the group in brainstorming creates completely new ideas. You might see only one way to accomplish what you want— and it may not be feasible based on your location, finances, or experience level. The group will help come up with alternate paths that are feasible right now wherever you are stationed.

> *The group helps you learn to live in the magical world of "possibility thinking."*

- You gain courage from the group. The group members provide a sounding board for your doubts and fears and support you in pushing past them, in both practical and concrete ways, and at an emotional level. Sometimes group members physically go along to provide moral support during a challenging task. As Cheryl Richardson says, "Groups are like Jell-O molds. They hold you up until you can stand on your own."
- The group acts as your own personal cheering squad. When you succeed at something, your group helps you celebrate. When you are feeling down, it helps to be around "up" people who can remind you that you won't always feel this way. As one woman said, "The reason groups work so well is that not everyone is depressed at the same time."
- Your group provides additional "antennae." Since your group members all know your dream, they bring in articles, contacts, and information for you that they run across—information that you might never have discovered yourself.
- The group helps you learn to live in the magical world of "possibility thinking." As you see others move toward what they want and succeed, you get inspired and motivated to take action yourself.

Is this type of team only for people trying to run their own business? Not at all! It doesn't matter what your dreams or goals are—they can be personal, parenting, spiritual, physical, financial, educational, whatever! They can be small or large, short-term or long-term. The group is just a means to get—and keep—you moving toward something you want. The best part is you have a lot of fun, laughter, and great conversation in the process!

So many of us as military spouses feel that our dreams have to stay on the back burner as long as we are moving constantly with the military—or as long as the kids are still growing—or until we become more motivated. But that isn't true. We can all move toward what we want—with help.

As army spouse Monica Dixon says, "My Mastermind group saved my life. We focused on Problem—Solution, Problem—Solution, No Whining!"

Mary Styron's Story

One Thursday morning I found myself driving over German hills look-ing for a town I couldn't even pronounce. I was apprehensive. I just met Kathie sitting at an AWAG conference. She called a few days ago, caught me at a moment of weakness and asked me if I wanted to attend a meeting of her "success group." Yeah, right.

So there I was, driving to this 11 a.m. meeting, picturing group hugs and the word "empowerment" hanging in the air like a battle cry. My husband admonished me that morning, "The first hint of man-bashing or femi-nazism and run like the wind."

I arrived at Kathie's house and was greeted ominously by whole kernel bran muffins and tea. Tea. I am strictly coffee, black, lotsa caffeine. Those little hairs on the back of my neck stood up and wiggled. I braced myself for crystals and incense.

The clock struck 11; the polite chatter ceased; the smiles disap-peared. A kitchen timer was placed in the center of the table with reverence. Kathie explained the process. Each of us had ten minutes to talk about ourselves—our goals, our frustrations, and our needs. The next ten minutes were to be spent in discussion and feedback. I was getting a little confused. She sounded so businesslike, not "new-agey" at all.

Gail was first. I imagined that she would bare her soul, bash her man, and blame society or the military. She began talking about the business that she had started here in Germany. Business was so good she had to rent a stall at the PX. I was agog. This woman was telling me about positive things. She went on to talk about the books she was writing!

Kathie's turn. This woman is a one-person enterprise. Neither woman ever said "empowerment." They both adore their husbands. They both took charge of their lives.

My first "success group" meeting ended, I bounced back to my car and raced home, listing dreams, formulating plans and discovering possibilities. I was challenged to determine what I really wanted to do with my life. I have rarely missed a meeting of my success group since that first one almost two years ago. The group has changed from a few timid women, quite unsure of their direction, into a bunch of

well-focused individuals. We are housewives, mothers, single profes-
sionals and Army officers. We have little in common but much to learn
from each other.

The group I so reluctantly joined has done wonders for me . . . the
most important of which is accountability. I could resolutely tell my
husband "Tomorrow I will do X" and never make a move to make
that resolution come true. I could stare at my dimpled thighs all day
long and swear the Nordic Trak to be my best friend, and never walk
those two blocks to the gym. I could envision my dream vocation at
every pause and not open a book to find out "how." But, tell a group
of tenacious women "I'm going to get it done before the next meet-
ing" . . . and I'll do it or die trying!

This group has taught me the power of networking, the beauty
of friendship, the strength of dreams and the satisfaction of getting
things done.

So, what about you? Interested? Do you want to start your own group? We would love to help anyone else who wants to start a support group, Dare to Dream Team, whatever you choose to call it. (Kathie's group in Corvallis called themselves the Big Group because they wanted to learn to live Big!)

Here's what we can do to help:

- We have a detailed handout spelling out what these groups are and how to start and run a meeting. Go to the Life Skills articles at www.military spousehelp.com to download the Dare to Dream Team handout for free.
- We are happy to answer your questions as you get going with your group, to give you ideas of exercises, to brainstorm resources and contacts for whatever dreams your group members have (we are really good at that and love to do it). In some cases, with your permission of course, we might ask our ezine audience for additional ideas.
- We want to hear your stories as your groups develop. They might just be things we can include in an article or a future book.

Ask for What You Want

When Gail Howerton, Heidelberg's Recreation Center director, coordinated a trip to Nepal, Kris Shelstad, an army spouse, really wanted to go. However, she had just started a new job and knew that her boss wouldn't let her take a two-week leave so soon.

"Why does it all have to come at once," she complained to her husband.

"Why couldn't the job be starting after the trip instead of right now?" At some point, he got tired of listening to her and passed on these words of wisdom. "Here you are complaining because your boss won't let you go," he said, "and you haven't even asked him. Why don't you ask him before you complain?"

She did ask him and he happily granted her leave without pay. She got to start the job *and* go to Nepal. Because she asked.

We keep Kris in mind whenever we really want something but we expect the answer will be no. It's amazing how often we decide what the other person's response will be without ever giving them the chance to speak. We'll never know how many opportunities we miss out on simply because we don't ask.

There are important things to consider in asking for what you want.

- Be specific. If you tell someone you are looking for a job, it would be hard for that person to help out. But if you specifically say, "I'm looking for contacts in the hospitality industry in the Washington area," they just might be able to give you the contacts you need.
- Be persistent. As is said in the marketing world, "Remember that you have to keep asking because 'No' often doesn't mean 'No.' It often just means 'No, not now.'" Caroline, an air force spouse learned this in marketing her writing. She sent one query to *Military Lifestyle* magazine every year for four years in a row. She knew it was a good article idea specifically targeted to the audience of that publication. The responses indicated that the timing just wasn't right, not that the idea was wrong for them. On the fourth try, the editor bought it. In the sales world they say that it takes eight sales calls to make the sale. Keep asking.
- Get support to help you ask. This is why the Dare to Dream Team concept works so well. When you have a hard time asking for what you want, your team can help you clarify it, help you practice asking, and sometimes even go along to lend moral support when you ask. They can provide the extra "kick in the pants" you need to force you to ask. Whenever you keep putting off asking for something you want, your group will call you on it.
- Ask as if you expect to get it. Expect a yes rather than a no and you likely will manifest one. It certainly changes the way you ask—your word use and tone of voice and body language. These factors impact the way you are perceived by the other person, which might just impact their decision.

For anyone who has trouble asking, we recommend the book, *The Aladdin Factor,* by Jack Canfield and Mark Victor Hansen. It's full of inspirational examples, tips and techniques. We kept underlining stories and writing notes in the margin as they reminded us of things we've wanted to ask for but hadn't had the guts to do so. Reading the amazing results others have had gives you motivation to try for yourself.

Can we tell you that you will always get what you ask for? Of course not. But we can predict what you will get if you fail to ask. As Patricia Fripp, a speaker and writer, says, "Everything in life is a sales situation... and the answer is no if you don't ask."

And Ask for Things That Affect All of Us

Often things happen to us in this military life that really don't make sense at all, things that affect other military spouses, not just us. In those cases, asking for what we want has an even wider scope if we manage to get something changed for everyone.

The Army's Family Action Plan (AFAP) program is a great example of that. Every year the community members of every post get to raise top concerns, asking for what they want changed. Many of those issues get solved locally. Others are raised to the Department of Army level. In fact, since the program started in 1983 no fewer than 82 changes have been made to legislation, 130 revisions made to policy and regulations, and 140 programs or services improved, partially because of AFAP. Things have changed for the better for all of us—because someone asked!

Another example that we should all know about as military spouses is the National Military Family Association (NMFA). NMFA was organized in 1969 as the National Military Wives Association by a group of wives and widows. At that time, if you were married to the military and your spouse died in retirement, his retirement pay stopped. You got nothing. Because of the efforts of these women, the Survivor Benefit Plan came into being.

Since then NMFA, a non-profit association, continues to educate military families about our rights, benefits, and services. They also promote and protect the interests of military family members by influencing the development and implementation of legislation and policies affecting all of us. NMFA really is our voice to Congress.

So many of the benefits we take for granted came about because of NMFA. Here are a few:

- the comprehensive dental plan for active duty families,
- student travel allowances for families stationed overseas,
- increased active duty survivor benefits,
- Cost of Living Allowance (COLA) for service members stationed in areas in CONUS with exceptionally high cost of living,
- adoption expense reimbursement for active duty military families.

Currently, NMFA is pushing for research to help the services better understand how to help military members transition back from war, to help them and their families adjust and deal with post-deployment problems.

We've recently heard of another spouse trying to make a change in a policy that is unfair to all military spouses. Have you ever left a job due to a military move and left retirement monies behind? This often happens to military spouses as we don't get to stay in a job long enough to be vested in our retirement account. Add to that the fact that you aren't eligible to contribute to a regular IRA during years you are covered by an employer retirement plan and you are doubly shorted of retirement funds.

Darcy Waris is a marine corps spouse and former human resources director who is working to change that unfair situation for all military spouses. She is trying to gather support for "MS-RISA"—the Military Spouse Retirement Income Security Act, which is in its infancy of being written and trying to find sponsors on Capital Hill. Her hope is a law requiring companies to fully vest military spouses who quit their jobs as a result of PCS orders, so they receive 100 percent of their retirement benefits from the plans in which they participate. Darcy used to manage pension plans, so has a good understanding of this area—and has had to give up retirement benefits twice herself.

> *Change happens because someone chose to believe that change was possible.*

When we mention this initiative to others we often hear, "That will never happen!" We expect many other initiatives have triggered that same reaction in the past, initiatives that have since become reality, resulting in positive change for all of us. That kind of change happens because someone chose to believe that change was possible and stepped out with possibility thinking to see what they could do.

Action Steps
- Download the Dare to Dream Team handout.
- Start talking to people about the team concept to get your own going.
- Write us with any questions.

Resources
Free Dare to Dream Team how-to details at our website, www.military spousehelp.com (Life Skills articles section).

Girls Night Out, by Tamara Kreinin and Barbara Camens.

National Military Family Association, Inc. 2500 North Van Dorn Street, Suite 102, Alexandria, VA 22302-1601; 703-931-6632, fax 703-931-4600; www.nmfa.org.

Teamworks: Building Support Groups that Guarantee Success, by Barbara Sher and Annie Gottleib (1991).

The Aladdin Factor, by Jack Canfield and Mark Victor Hansen (1995).

Wishcraft: *How to Get What You Really Want*, by Barbara Sher with Annie Gottleib (2003).

Chapter 13

Ask for Help, Accept Help, Offer Help in Challenging Times

Acknowledge That Extra Help Is Necessary

Ask For—And Accept Help—When You Need It

A few years ago, Cherie, a marine spouse, found out—after the fact—that a dear friend had been going through serious depression. She hid it well, always putting on a positive front. None of her close friends knew. They all felt terrible when they found out. There was so much they would have happily done to lighten her load—if they'd only known!

Have you ever been there? You know how that feels. So turn it around. If you need help, and you don't let anyone know, you cheat your friends of the opportunity to help.

Most military spouses happily step in to help others. You really do reap benefits for yourself when you help others even though that isn't why you help. But when it comes to being able to ask for help for ourselves, we are among the worst.

Holly fits right into that mold—always reaching out to help others but not as good about asking for help when she needs it. As a single mom with twin infants while her husband was deployed, that trait came to a head one day. One of her four-month-old twins was sick and not sleeping for days on end. Holly was so sleep deprived she couldn't think straight.

Julie Woods and Beverly Young, two army wives who lived on Holly's street, stopped by that day to see how Holly was doing. In just minutes they realized Holly was at the end of her rope. They decided to step in and take over with the kids and told Holly to go to bed. Julie even got someone to fill in for her at work so she could help Holly.

Of course, Holly started protesting immediately. What is it about us that we can't just accept needed help graciously? When someone really wants to help you, thank him or her and accept the help.

We've heard many stories during the Iraq deployment of spouses who had to go into the hospital for a procedure or even a birth, who didn't let anyone know. They went on their own, in some cases with small children in tow, rather than asking help of their friends and neighbors. Everyone around them felt terrible after they found out.

We think this sometimes happens because we all know people who ask for help all the time, too much of the time, the ones who seem to expect everything to be done for them. You've all met someone like that. They are the ones complaining all the time, demanding that the military take care of them. They are the ones complaining about the military but not even accessing the resources that are provided. You don't want to be like that, so you end up not asking for the help that is reasonable to ask for, help that you really need. Think about this. You know how we joke about people who won't ask for directions when they are lost? Well, it's just as ridiculous to not ask for help when you need it.

Pay It Forward

Remember, when you think, "How can I repay you?" You don't have to. You can help someone else in the future. That's how this military life works. You probably can't repay the person who helps you, but you can pay it forward by helping someone else at a later date. Dorothy Wilhelm is an army widow and mother of six with two sons and one son-in-law who are career military. She learned the lesson about forward payment early in her military life.

Here's her story:

It was Christmas. I was alone in the maternity ward of a big Air Force Base hospital in California, facing months in bed as the result of a complicated pregnancy. My husband had taken our infant daughter to get settled with his mother until the new baby was born—and doctors weren't optimistic. They told us the expected child almost surely wouldn't live. I lay in the starkly furnished hospital ward, with twenty-two women, all happy new mothers, and I was not able to keep back the tears. I was only twenty-two years old. Without warning, a small tornado whirled into the room. Her name was Mary Ann and her husband was part of my husband's Army ordnance company. That was all I knew. I'd been on her mind, she said. She couldn't bear to think of my spending Christmas alone, she told me. I wasn't too crazy about the idea myself, I admitted.

"You're coming home with me," Mary Ann announced in a voice that brooked no argument.

This young mother had plenty of other things to do during the hectic holiday season with her own three small children and a dog, but she took care of me, confined to bed, as if it was the one thing she wanted to do. As in all good Christmas stories, her family made room for the stranger in its midst.

Despite the wise medical opinion, my baby didn't die. In the spring I wrapped my healthy new son in a blue blanket and went back to say thank you to Mary Ann. We already had orders to a new post, so I'd have no chance to repay her or even to see her again. "I just don't know how I can pay you back," I said. Mary Anne looked at me as if I weren't quite bright, something I was to become used to over the years ahead.

"You can't do anything for me," she said. "You'll do it for somebody else."

Those six words have followed me down the years—the motto for military families everywhere—we do it for somebody else."

(One time reprint rights granted by Dorothy Wilhelm. This column originally appeared in the Tacoma News Tribune on December 5, 2001. Contact Dorothy (www.itsnevertoolate.com).

Be Specific in Your Offers of Help

When you do offer help, don't just say, "What can I do to help?" A lot of us can't easily verbalize what we need. That question often results in the polite but untrue answer of, "Oh nothing, I'm fine."

Be specific. Here are a couple of Holly's favorites from that time of deployment.

- "I made dinner for my family and I made an extra plate for you. Can I bring it over?"
- "I'm going to the commissary. Do you need milk or anything?" What a gift. Getting two babies ready and shopping at the commissary was an insurmountable task at times, especially when it was just for one or two items.

Another army spouse, Linda Beougher, dealing with challenging medical problems, shares some things that helped her during that time.

- Other parents took my two girls for play dates or sleepovers so I could get the sleep I was supposed to be getting to heal.
- Since I wasn't able to drive and my husband couldn't take any more time away from work, friends drove me to doctor appointments and drove the girls to their activities so they could keep some routine going.
- Neighbors gave us dinner coupons for local restaurants—especially helpful were those restaurants that delivered.

Asking for help and offering effective help aren't always automatic skills we have. Like many other skills, we develop them over time.

Access the Help That Is Available

Part of asking for help is asking about and accessing the help provided by the services. One of the biggest frustrations of the people coordinating family programs is the small number of people who take advantage of them. Check with your family support center, read your post newspaper, and pay attention to the flyers on post. Don't assume you know everything that is available just because you've been married to the military for a while. New programs arise regularly.

Here are some recent examples:

- Many posts/bases provide some free respite care, taking care of children so that mom or dad get time for themselves during deployment.
- Some units have overnight "lock-ins" with activities, fun, and supervision for the kids so mom or dad gets one night to themselves.
- Operation Purple, a joint effort of Sears and the National Military Family Association, provided free summer camp for children of deployed military during the summers of 2004/2005/2006, hopefully to be repeated in future years.
- Operation Homefront at operationhomefront.net, where communities are stepping in to help the families of deployed military with everything from car repairs to home repairs to Internet connected computers.

Make Use of Military OneSource—One Incredible Resource

Hopefully, you've heard about Military OneSource.com by now, but if not, this is a key military benefit to know about. And even if you've heard of it, you might not appreciate the magnitude of help available to you through this service. We bet most military spouses don't. We sure didn't—until recently.

A comment by a marine corps spouse at a recent workshop opened our eyes.

As we brainstormed one spouse's dream in our workshop, which entailed pursuing a degree, ideas flew onto the flipchart paper, including ideas on how to research scholarships and grants. Her reply to these ideas was, "Well, that's great, but that in itself can be a fulltime job, doing that kind of research, and I'm fully loaded with work as it is during this deployment." At that, another woman piped up.

"Call Military OneSource and they'll do the research for you," she said. "They will?!" we asked a bit incredulously? "Yes, we were told that at a briefing about Military OneSource last week. They will research grants and scholarships based on your specific situation."

We admit we found that a bit hard to believe, so we checked it out. It's true. While asking the Department of Defense policy section this specific question, we also requested examples of the kinds of information individuals have asked Military OneSource to provide. Here's a sample:

- Childcare availability in a particular area. The counselors on the end of the phone can provide a list of providers on and off base as well as whether or not they are licensed. (There are online locators for things like childcare, eldercare, massage practitioners as well.)
- School reports that provide teacher/student ratios at schools and SAT scores of the schools located near a particular base.
- Exceptional family member services available in an area.
- All types of parenting issues, such as potty training for toddlers.
- Where to get car repairs done.
- Landlord/tenant problems.
- Relationship problem solving.
- Dealing with relocation stress.
- Adoption assistance.
- Gambling addiction or eating disorders.
- Pet care availability.

Families can request a Know Your Neighborhood guide, a zip code based report provides information about any community they are in or moving to.

You can also get six free confidential in-person counseling sessions through this service (this is available to the military member, spouse, or child). We're also impressed by the kind of information and resources available on their website, things like online self-assessments and free CDs on stress and deployments, free TurboTax software, free home baby proofing kits.

Another thing to be aware of is the fact that simultaneous translation is available over the telephone for about one hundred fifty different languages. You can even fax in a doctor's bill or utility bill for translation (and the fax service is available free through family service centers on base).

What a gift to individuals! And what a gift to unit leaders, Family Readiness Group Leaders, Key Volunteers, Ombudsmen, and Family Service staff members. Now when you are asked a question or faced with a situation you have no experience with, you have an instant place to turn to get helpful information.

This service is available online or by phone 24/7 365 days a year so it's available to families who are living away from a military installation. It solves the problem of family members who work and can't access the 9 to 5 services available on base. The individuals who answer the phone are all master's level consultants and the service can be used anonymously. The policy is that a telephone must be answered within three rings, and you don't have to jump through the kind of "push 1 for, push 2 for," hoops some companies make you deal with. Military OneSource is available to all active duty, guard, and reserve members (regardless of status), their family members, installation helping agencies, Individual Ready Reserve (IRR), and Department of Defense civilians who live overseas.

Talk about an easy and accessible way to ask for the help you need!

Get Professional Help When Necessary

There is another kind of help that needs to be discussed—help when you are depressed. It's something we don't talk about openly enough. The fact is that people who need help—who need counseling or therapy or maybe even drug therapy—often won't ask for it because of military culture and reality. In some cases people don't even recognize they are depressed and that help is available.

"I just couldn't get myself out of bed," she told us. "I dragged through each day doing the bare minimum of things that had to be done. I procrastinated on everything, even important things. I just couldn't seem to care." Cheryl is an air force spouse describing her experience with depression. "I kept thinking, what's wrong with me?" She went on, "I have nothing to be depressed about. My husband isn't deployed to Iraq like so many of my neighbor's husbands are. If anyone deserves to feel depressed right now, it's them, not me. I have a good life, a great relationship with my husband, good friends. What do I have to be depressed about?" That kind of thinking kept her from asking for help for months. Finally her uncontrollable crying, constant insomnia, and feelings of failure and helplessness drove her to get help.

The National Institute of Mental Health estimates nineteen million adult Americans suffer from depression during any one-year period. Two thirds of those do not get the help they need. Eighty percent of people who are treated show significant improvement, but many people do not even recognize that they have a condition that can be treated, or even if they do, many won't go for help.

There is a social stigma. As Dr. Susan Fletcher, who has worked with adult depression in private practice for more than twelve years says, "Many people grew up hearing 'Get over it—life's not that hard.'"

Depression is one of those things many of us don't talk about, in society at large, but especially in our military world. People who need help often won't ask for it because of military culture. This applies to both the spouse and the military member.

"If I go for counseling it goes on my record and affects my promotability and security clearance." The Defense Department study on post-traumatic stress and other mental disorders among soldiers and marines returning from Iraq and Afghanistan reported this attitude in the *New England Journal of Medicine*. Of the troops whose responses indicated they had a mental disorder, between 23 to 40 percent sought professional help. Troops said seeking mental health care would kill their careers—that their command climate was to just "suck it up."

The civilian spouse of a military member has related fears. "If I go for counseling it will go on my husband's record and affect the way he is seen by superiors—'Can't you control your family? If you have problems at home, you most likely aren't as effective a leader or team player at work either.' And that can affect our family livelihood. Am I really prepared for that?"

Plus there's the whole confidentiality thing. The on-post community is small. Who is going to go for counseling on post if they fear their neighbors will know about it? Yes, we know that counselors are supposed to maintain confidentiality and we expect most do, but that doesn't mean we don't still have the fear that a counselor won't. It may be an irrational fear but who ever said you are fully rational, especially when you are depressed?

For the military member and many males, there is the whole macho/strength factor—with depression seen as weakness. In fact, the National Institute of Mental Health started a "Real Men, Real Depression" campaign to bring more attention to that subject in society.

We have a similar challenge as military spouses. We have a bit of the "pioneer" mentality. We say, "We are strong and can handle anything thrown our way. At least that is what everyone else seems to manage, so what is wrong with me?" "No matter how bad my situation is, there is another military spouse who has it worse. . . . I've had to move too much, every three years, sometimes after only one or two. But that family had to move three times in two years! . . . My husband deployed into a danger zone for six months. But our neighbor's been in three major deployments *and* did an unaccompanied tour in Korea. . . . I'm struggling here being the 'single' parent of two babies. But my neighbor is managing with five kids while her spouse is deployed." "How can I complain? What's wrong with me that I can't handle it? Why can't I just 'snap out of it,' have a positive attitude, get moving?"

People who need help often won't ask for it because of military culture.

There may well be spouses who move smoothly through this military life. We've met them—so have you. They seem to take it all in stride. In fact, some thrive on crisis and change. Which of course makes us wonder, why can't we?

Kathie's friend Claire says, "Don't compare your inners to their outers." We never really know what's going on in someone else's life and mind while we know our own intimately. We judge how others are doing based on our perceptions of how they are doing, based on what they show to the outside world. Who knows what the reality of their lives really is?

Another thing to consider is this. We are all so different in our energy levels, in our basic mood levels, in our organization habits, and in past experiences that have taught us or not taught us effective coping skills. Some people inherit a tendency to depression. Just because one person can easily handle a tough situation doesn't mean we all can.

Depression can happen because of many different things, from life experiences to chemical imbalance. Experts tell us that psychological stresses that can bring on depression include loss or major life changes—positive as well as negative ones. Well, if anyone faces major life changes and loss on a recurring basis, it's military spouses! The experts also say that most people will have signs of depression at some time in their lives. It can be a minor illness that lasts a short time and goes away by itself. It can be a major illness that severely limits how you function, and requires treatment.

In 2006, concerned by rising stress levels in the ranks, the Defense Department started an online self-screening program in hopes that anonymity will help some service members and their spouses overcome reluctance to confront possible mental health problems. The Mental Health Self-Assessment program is offered online at www.militarymentalhealth.org and assesses answers to questions about recent behavior and mood swings. If the responses indicate possible trouble, the program suggests options for seeking help.

We can also make confidential calls to Military OneSource for advice and referral for six sessions of free counseling off-post.

The first step is to know the signs of depression so we might recognize it in ourselves, in our spouses, or in our friends. Sometimes when a person is deeply depressed, they can't take action to get help. It can mean a friend stepping in to help them get the help they need.

If more people are open about their need for counseling it will become more accepted. Hopefully, like other outdated "rules" of military life, we can eventually get rid of the stigma that keeps people from getting the help they need, spouses and military alike.

As for Cheryl, she finally saw her doctor who prescribed a mild antidepressant medication. With that, increased exercise, and getting involved in activities again, things shifted. She said, "I feel like I have my life back!"

Recognize the Signs of Depression
These can all be symptoms of depression:

- feeling down, blue, hopeless, sad, or irritable,
- no longer feeling pleasure when you do things that would usually be fun,
- having low self-esteem ("I'm not a competent person."), negative think-

ing ("I'll never feel better."), and trouble concentrating,

- feeling less energy,
- seeing changes in your appetite, weight, sleeping patterns, or having more physical pain,
- feeling bad enough that you are having trouble doing your normal activities at work or at home,
- abuse of alcohol or drugs.

Based on the above list, if you answer yes to the following three questions, it's time to get help.

1. Do you have some or all of the symptoms listed above?
2. Have you had them for two weeks or more?
3. Are they getting in the way of your normal life at home, school, or work?

Resources

Finding My Way: A Teen's Guide to Living with a Parent Who Has Experienced Trauma, by Michelle D. Sherman, Ph.D., and DeAnne M. Sherman (2005).

National Institute of Mental Health. www.nimh.nih.gov.

We found Dr. Fletcher's CD on Adult Depression to be clear and helpful. www.HearSusan.com/products.asp.

Military OneSource, www.militaryonesource.com—User ID: military; password: onesource.

MilitaryOneSource:

U.S.: 1-800-342-9647

Overseas: 800-3429-6477

Overseas collect: 484-530-5908

Access codes can be found online.

(Besides the availability of free confidential in-person counseling, the website has many resources about depression, from articles to free CDs.)

New Light on Depression: Help, Hope, and Answers for the Depressed and Those Who Love Them, by Harold George Koenig (2004).

Tricare will connect you with a counselor to talk with outside the military base— all confidential. Like Military OneSource counseling, referrals are strictly confidential unless you are seeking to hurt yourself or others. Then it is their obligation to break your confidentiality and to involve others to help you.

Chapter 14

The Richness of Military Life

Look at the Benefits as Well as
the Challenges of This Lifestyle

W e've told you how we both spent the early years of our military married life complaining about the challenges. But looking back on that life now we wouldn't give it up. Why? Because we have both gained so much from our experiences. We believe we've grown more than we might have if we'd stayed settled in one place. We hear that from so many of the spouses we talk to.

Of course we think it's important to acknowledge and address the challenges of this life. It's just as important to make sure we acknowledge and take advantage of the benefits this life offers us. And it provides many positive things. As army spouse Kris says, "It is so overwhelming at times, especially the moves, but as my Grandma used to say, 'I'll take the roller coaster over the carousel any day!'"

Or as Brenda Pace and Carol McGlothlin, authors of *Medals Above My Heart* say, "Like the wives of great military leaders of the past, present day military wives experience challenges that stretch their physical, emotional, and spiritual resources. While it is an honor to serve her soldier, airman, marine, or sailor as he defends the freedom of America, it is not without sacrifice. They receive no medals from their country but receive a reward greater than any medal. They reap the benefits of personal character and leadership development, adventure, relationships, and opportunities for service."

Here are the benefits mentioned over and over again as we interviewed other military spouses.

Cherish Patriotism, Pride, and Esprit de Corps

Neither one of us can attend a military parade, listen to the Star Spangled banner being played in a military theater, or watch a reunion ceremony without choking up or dabbing away tears.

One thing our military life has given us is a deep sense of pride in the men and women who serve in the military. You really get to see how professional and dedicated they are. And as spouses, you are part of that, of the dedication, professionalism and sacrifices made for our country and to help other countries. Military spouses are part of something much bigger than themselves, something most other people never get to experience.

When we've been involved with deployments, especially, we've felt the deep connection to group. There is a sisterhood among military spouses bonded by our experiences. We both have many civilian friends who we admire, but we don't know too many who have had to overcome and thrive in the kinds of challenges that military spouses deal with regularly.

We love each of our soldiers, airmen, sailors, marines, and coast guardsmen and are proud to be standing beside them. Cherish that sense of pride, patriotism, and esprit de corps.

Get to Know Our Country

For many people, the first chance to really get to know this vast country of ours is when they retire, invest in an RV, and hit the road. As military spouses we have that opportunity much sooner.

"One highlight of military life for me," says army spouse Linda Beougher, "is moving around the country and finding out what we truly like about an area as we discover it through 'infant eyes.' I lived in places for short periods of time and would delve into the museums, monuments, history, etc., and was often told by locals that I knew their home better than they did."

We have the advantage of knowing we will be moving on. Whereas locals always feel like "I can get to that another time," we know we might not. Add to that the fact that locals tend to travel in circumscribed paths. One advantage to being new to a place is how much you discover, as you get lost regularly while learning your way around.

Many military families have discovered parts of the country they prefer over where they originally lived, something they might never had done without military moves.

Seek Out Unique Opportunities, Compliments of Uncle Sam

During a workshop in Germany, as we had folks running around to get ideas and resources for the dreams they have, one woman's label read "Horse farm."

She clarified for us that she eventually wanted horses—something not possible for her in Germany. *Au contraire,* we thought to ourselves. "Have you connected with any local German horse people?" we asked. No, she hadn't. She was just waiting until they moved back to the United States. That might be three years of not pursuing her passion.

As military spouses, it's key to realize that opportunities exist everywhere—even in Germany or Japan or Turkey, even in a remote site in rural Georgia, even when you think you are stuck in the "middle of nowhere." The challenge is to look for and take advantage of those opportunities. Many of them are not just amazing opportunities they are experiences you will find nowhere else in the world.

Ask the questions. "What is available here? What is unique to this place that I can use in my dream development? How can I make use of this situation?" Asking those questions sets off light bulbs in your head, at least much more so than when you stick to the mantra of, "If only we weren't sent here. . . ." (We know; we've tried it both ways!)

Here are some ideas that made this woman's face light up in our workshop: Interview horse places where she's living. Enlist the help of a military spouse who speaks German. Write an article for the post paper for all those other horse-lovers. It's a win/win. She'll learn tips on managing horse farms, make valuable contacts, and find places to ride. She'll get to experience how the horse world in a foreign country differs from the one she knows. She'll provide a service to other military members. And she'll provide marketing to German horse stables, connecting our two communities.

Turning our thinking around about military life can open amazing opportunities all paid for by someone else. Rather than complain about another move (okay, we give you time to complain about the moving process itself), we can thank Uncle Sam for a free trip to do research for our dreams and our lives.

> *"What is available here? What is unique to this place that I can use in my dream development?" and thank Uncle Sam for making our dream fulfillment and life richer than if we'd stayed in one place.*

Think like Sandee Payne, author of *That Military House, Move it, Organize it and Decorate it.* She decided to think of PCS (Permanent Change of Station) in a more positive light by changing the acronym to Positive Change in Surroundings.

Sound Pollyanna-ish? Well, what's the alternative? Wishing you lived someplace else doesn't get you very far. We know. We've tried that. Besides, have you noticed how limited your old friends' lives seem—the ones who've never lived any place different or traveled anywhere? The ones who hang out in the same places and talk about the same things they did in high school? The ones who are still working at the same companies where they've worked for the past twenty years, including many who hate their jobs? There are advantages to moving around. Why not focus on the benefits instead of focusing on what's missing? What we choose to focus on really is our choice to make.

Army spouse Linda Beougher made that choice begrudgingly at first but now sees the benefit. "I've found a harp teacher relatively nearby everywhere we've lived," she says. "At first I was a bit perturbed that I kept having to switch teachers so frequently, but over the years I've learned that each mentor had different strengths. It has been a true blessing to work with many very talented individuals each teaching me something different."

Consider this:

- What artist wouldn't love to live in Europe or the Far East and interact with international artists?
- What master's student couldn't add depth and dimension to his or her thesis by interviewing topic matter experts in other states and countries?
- What cook wouldn't love to try foods and cooking techniques in places as varied as Okinawa, Korea, and Turkey?

What's your dream and where are you located? Write us or email us and we'll see what ideas we can come up with to take full advantage of unique possibilities in this latest trip provided to you, courtesy of the U.S. Government.

Take the Opportunity to Reinvent Yourself

During a workshop for marine spouses in Okinawa, one woman told us this story. She had been working in city management at one location and had just been offered a promotion. Of course, that is when they got orders to move. A coworker said to her, "How do you deal with that? Just as you have this great opportunity, you have no choice but to give it up and move on." We were impressed with the woman's reply.

"Well, that is one way to look at it," she said, "but just think, how many times in your life have you had the chance to reinvent yourself? As military spouses we get that chance on a regular basis."

We've often had this discussion with civilian friends who have lived in one place forever. It can be very hard for someone in that situation to take on a new project or career. Friends and neighbors already have a set perception of who you are and what you are capable of. When we move to a new place, those preconceived ideas don't exist. We start fresh. You can even take on a new style as you move. We know of one marine corps child who chose to change his name with one move.

So, think of each new move as an opportunity. You may choose to reinvent yourself. What a gift!

Discover New Interests

Kathie's Story

My husband Greg and I are avid sea kayakers. We even own our own kayaks and have kayaked all over, in Alaska, in Baja, on lakes and rivers and bays. We have many plans for future trips.

My family and childhood friends from the suburbs of Northern Virginia find that hard to believe. They knew me as a shy, quiet, non-athletic bookworm and a chicken when it comes to physical activities.

If we hadn't moved with the military to the Northwest, I doubt I would have ever tried kayaking or hiking or gardening, all things that are central to my world these days. Every time I walk along or kayak in the water in the Northwest, with views of the Olympics and Mount Rainier, I thank my lucky stars that I no longer live in the suburbs of [Washington,] DC, as most of my high school friends still do. I've discovered new interests here as well as an environment that "makes my soul sing" as my friend Sarah says.

We hear the same from so many military spouses. They often discover passions and places through this military life experience that they would never have had the opportunity to experience in most other lives. We've talked to spouses who became enamored of riding horses when they were stationed in Texas. Others have taken up surfing in California, water-skiing in Alabama, flower arranging in Japan, exotic cooking in Turkey, or antiquing in Georgia.

Moving around so frequently opens you up to many new opportunities. Much of it is free or inexpensive because it's provided through the military. Open the pages of any post/base newspaper and browse through the available classes and trips.

Note about exploring:

Don't limit yourself to what is available on post, especially when you live in a foreign country. You probably know military families who hated their assignments overseas. Often you find out after talking with them further that they never left their base or post! Sure, it's a little scary to go off-post in a country where you don't speak the language and don't know the customs. Take advantage of the orientation programs offered in many military communities overseas. Befriend a military spouse who does know the language or at least already knows her way around a bit. Plus it's always easier to go exploring with someone else unless you happen to be one of those who loves to do that on your own.

"I think the biggest benefit to military life is all the travel!" says marine spouse Lori Cleymans. She describes how she did not enjoy Okinawa at first, until she started to explore and learn about the culture, language, and traditions. "While in Okinawa, we took a trip to China and Kyoto, Japan. Again, we would have never done that while living in the states. We went to China as part of an ITT tour group and it was a blast! I saw the Great Wall, the Forbidden City, the terracotta soldiers, and so many wonderful sites."

When you live overseas, travel and learning options are even more exotic and more affordable than here in the states. Take advantage of those inexpensive Morale Welfare and Recreation trips and tours and learn about great opportunities from other military spouses. In Germany, for example, be sure to read a copy of *Never a Dull Moment* as soon as you arrive. This book is updated regularly by military spouses and sold as a fundraiser for the American Women's Activities Germany. It lists places to shop, eat, and stay throughout Germany. You can get a similar book for Italy. Check with the spouse club and with other military spouses you meet when you get to a new assignment to find out what's available there. Ask other military spouses and families for suggestions on what to do and see, where to eat out, what activities you or your kids might enjoy. We've both had great experiences we would have missed if we hadn't had the advice and guidance of other military spouses.

Listen to what marine spouse Amy Fetzer says: "I've been able to do things that most people never get the chance to do, just because I was married to a Marine. How many people can say they've ridden in an Armored Personnel Carrier, rappelled down a cliff in Okinawa to scuba dive, or had lunch in a Chinese Junk floating on Fragrant Harbor in Hong Kong?"

Ask military spouses to list some of the highlights of their lives, and they often come up with activities that would have been difficult (or cost-prohibitive) to do in another environment. Here are some we heard:

- *Four-day hut-to-hut hike in Austria* provided inexpensively by MWR Heidelberg—awesome scenery that can only be accessed by hiking or mountain biking.
- *Attending an International Harp Conference in Prague.* "If we hadn't been living in Germany, an affordable train-ride away, I could never have done that. My U.S. harp colleagues are green with envy."

- *Running a marathon on the Great Wall of China!*
- *An all-inclusive family-oriented Centre Park resort in Germany.* "Better and more affordable than Disney world. I wish they had those in the United States. Best family vacation we ever had."
- *Swimming with the sharks in Hawaii.* "Okay, you are in a cage of course, but it's incredible."
- *A barge vacation in France.* "It was affordable for us because we could drive there from where we were stationed in Germany. We split the cost with other military families. We drove the barge and did our own cooking."
- *Touring Paris with my children.* "My children have vivid memories of the Louvre and Notre Dame. We camped to make the trip affordable but that added to the fun."
- *Having friends literally all over the world!*
- "Travel is more than the seeing of sights; it's a change that goes on, deep and permanent, in the ideas of living."—Miriam Beard

As military spouses, we grow and evolve as our personalities develop. You might move to Arizona or New Mexico and suddenly find you have a passion for Native American art. It's just an aspect of your personality that was waiting to be explored, that you might never have discovered staying in one place.

When Janette Thomas' husband was assigned to the Marine Corps' Mountain Warfare Training Center in Bridgeport, California, she knew her husband and boys were going to love this assignment. She knew she would hate it. For someone who used to work in shopping center management and who thrives in urban settings, a remote site in the mountains located two hours from the closest store of any size (and that being Target), this assignment loomed bleak.

Since she had to drive her sons to school every day in a forty-minute round trip, Janette started volunteering at the school. Her volunteer job turned into a paid position to create an art appreciation program for the school, something she had never considered getting involved in. Using the Internet to research ideas, she created a program that brought the students and her great joy. Now she's pursuing that line of work, something she would never have even thought of in the past. That assignment turned out to be a good one for her, as well as for her husband and kids.

Open the World to Your Kids

Hope Gibbs moved six times as a child because of her dad's naval career. Each move was an adventure for Hope and her sister because of their mother. "Mom always made it sound like wherever we were going was the best place on earth," says Hope. "She would research what interesting sights there were to see, and find out about youth groups, schools, and churches so that we would already feel a little at home by the time we got there."

Ask any military "brat" about his or her experiences growing up and you'll hear the negatives brought on by constant moves. But you'll hear about amazing opportunities as well, as experience greatly expanded each individual's world view to encompass the global community.

- "I got to take my elementary school photo in a kimono. Sure stands out from those other school photos."
- "We got to graduate from high school in the ruins of an ancient temple in Turkey."
- "I got to go on a student cruise with visits to Egypt and Morocco."
- "I attended a German–American school, which started my interest in international relations and gave me a good base on a second language."
- "My American friends are amazed that our family trips included places like Amsterdam, Paris, and hiking in Japan."

Some of the disadvantages of military life can turn into long-term advantages. Nancy was an extremely shy child who had a hard time dealing with change. Moving with the air force, starting new schools, and having to make new friends was always excruciating for her. She now sees those experiences as valuable skill-building ones that helped her to more easily step into new situations and create new communities as an adult.

As army spouse Linda says, "We were able to have our girls attend a German school for a while. They learned some of the German language and customs, but more im-

Some of the disadvantages of military life can turn into long-term advantages.

portantly it opened their minds to difference in the way other people think and do things—they learned that no one is correct, just different!"

Open Yourself to the World

You gain a lot from living in so many different states and foreign countries. You become more open to different customs and cultures than many of our countrymen who have never left the country or in many cases have never left their own states. You are more interested in international news and more aware of world situations, because your life has been and can always be closely affected by those situations. As the world community becomes more globally connected, this becomes more important to all of us.

We've noticed that our international experience allows us to hold our own in conversations with people of all levels and backgrounds, a definite plus in the business world. Many of the experiences we've been blessed with because of this military life are experiences that only the elite and rich have had access to in the past. We don't know about you, but much as we don't love the actual moving part of this life, we've loved the living in and experiencing so many different worlds. It's made our lives overall much richer.

Relish the Opportunity for Personal Growth

Susan Agustin, an army spouse, comes from a small town in Pennsylvania. "I guess it was a good place to grow up," she says, "but I'm glad I was able to leave and experience other things. . . . You become so empowered as you move with the military," she says. "You take on challenges, learn new things, and meet new people. It's amazing what you get to experience." Compared to the narrow lives of her peers back home, hers is rich indeed. "I wouldn't trade my life for any of theirs," she adds. We hope you end up saying exactly the same thing.

Action Steps

- Make a list of unique experiences you've had because of this military life. Any life highlights?
- Look at this current assignment with fresh eyes. What is unique to this place that you and your family might try? Check with the family service center and the recreation center on your post or base to find out what classes and trips are available. Ask other spouses what they recommend, those "not to miss" places and experiences.
- When you move to your next assignment, make finding some new experience a conscious proactive part of the moving plans.

Chapter 15

It's Time to Take Action
for Your Life

Start Today to Craft a Life That Works for You

---

*You can craft a life that works for you as you move with the
military, and it can be a rich, full, satisfying life. Start today!*

Deciding to pursue your dreams, be more joyful, have more energy and
balance are not "one time" activities. We don't want you to get the idea
that you have to take everything in this book and apply it right away.
That would be impossible. It would be like seeing a beautifully tended garden
and thinking, "I want to make mine look the same." Then you go out and weed
for hours until your garden looks great. The key is this. If you don't keep weeding in small amounts on a regular basis, it won't be long before your garden is
back to where it was when you started.

It is the same thing with your life. Negativity and imbalance can come
right back in if you don't keep weeding them out. If you continually return to
this book, read other inspirational articles and books, meet and spend time with
positive people, plan and schedule in the activities and people that are important to you, plan and take those Simple Joy breaks, and spend some alone time
in meditation and reflection, you'll keep those weeds at bay. Your life will be a
well-tended garden of delight.

We both made many of the changes we describe in this book over time,
over a *long* time, and we continue that lifelong process today. The key is to make
some conscious choices about what you want in your life and to take action
toward your vision, one step at a time. Don't wait for "some day." Start now.

Start out by identifying at least one area you'd like to make a change in. Maybe it's in your energy level or in your immediate environment. Maybe it's identifying what's important to you so you can set goals to work toward those things or maybe it's identifying some simple joys that you might add in immediately.

Here's what we know for sure. Once you figure out your priorities and start to set goals to take action in those areas, you'll see success. And once you see success with one small goal, you gain the motivation to move toward the next one. Taking action, taking responsibility for your life, and taking control of things you can control in a life full of things you can't control gives you great satisfaction. Identifying your interests and becoming engaged in life will change your experience of life itself.

> *Life is a process, which we need to enjoy as it unfolds. The joy really is in the journey, not in the final destination.*

You can craft an authentic life that works for *you* as you move with the military, and it can be a rich, full, satisfying life. Start today.

Resources

We share resources at the end of each section along with the ones we include here. But realize that it would be impossible for us to share every resource that might be specifically useful to each one of you. Certainly take advantage of the ones that do. We hope some of the ones we list will inspire you to locate others that fit your own unique needs and goals. Learn how to effectively search the web for resources, or find a friend who knows how to do that to show you. Get to know your reference librarian. They can help you find what you need and often have access to directories you can't access alone.

Books

We are convinced you can find a how-to book for whatever you want to do in life. Want to run a Bed and Breakfast? Read *The Complete Idiot's Guide to Running a Bed and Breakfast,* or one of about twenty other similar books. Want to home school your children? Read *Home Schooling: The Early Years: Your Complete Guide to Home School the 3 to 8 Year Old,* or one of about two hundred plus other books. Want to publish a nonfiction book? Read *The Shortest Distance Between You and a Published Book,* by Susan Page or many other books written for prospective authors.

Extended Learning Centers

Great resources available in many areas are extended learning centers, offered through universities or community colleges and organizations like Discovery U and Learning Annex. You can take concentrated one-evening courses on just about anything. Just as an example, here are a few courses listed in the latest Seattle area Discovery U catalog: Ebay 101: Selling/Buying Skills and Tips; Secrets of Unshakeable Self-Confidence; Become a Mystery Shopper; Improve Your Speaking Voice; Break into the Import/Export Business; How to Start a Greeting Card Business.

Associations

There is probably an association for whatever you want to do. As a speaker, Kathie can tell you how much her membership in the National Speakers Association shortened her learning curve about that business. Now the Pacific NW Writer's Association and other writer associations are helping her learn what she needs in the writing world. There are useful associations for non-career things as well as business/career things. Your membership gives you a quick way to connect with like-minded people in every new community as you move around the world. Gales Encyclopedia of Associations, available at most libraries, can steer you toward the professional association for you.

Specific Resources for Military Families

We obviously couldn't possibly cover everything you need to know for your military life in one book. Our focus obviously is on what you can do to craft the best life for you throughout the moves and deployments and other aspects of military life—how to take control of your own happiness in life—how to make conscious choices and take action.

The following are all important books written by military spouses. Find the ones that speak to you based on your current situation and interests.

Nonfiction Books—Some Highlights

E-mail to the Front, by Alesia Holliday (2003). Emails back and forth between the author and her husband, as well as thoughts about deployment and military life. You'll laugh out loud at experiences that will hit close to home, and cry at others in this open, honest view of our lives. One favorite line as she faces her first deployment: "Stop worrying! So I'm alone with a baby and a two-year old. I'm a tough trial lawyer, how hard can staying at home with two kids be? (*Note to Self:* The stupidest thing I've ever said in my entire life.)"

Going Overboard: The Misadventures of a Military Wife, by Sarah Smiley (2005). Reads like a novel as she describes the challenges of dealing with her husband's first deployment.

Heroes at Home: Help and Hope for America's Military Families, by Ellie

Kay (2002). Full of great ideas for dealing with deployments and military life in general with good parenting ideas included.

Jobs and the Military Spouse: Married, Mobile and Motivated for the New Job Market, Second Edition, by Janet I. Farley (2004). All the basics you need to know about the job search process and full of good resources. And for later in your military life, as you prepare to transition out, her *Military-to-Civilian Career Transition Guide* (2004) covers basics.

Married to the Military: A Survival Guide for Military Wives, Girlfriends, and Women in Uniform (2W3), by Meredith Leyva, founder of the website CinCHouse.com is easy to read and refer back to. We loved the "Did You Know" segments. For example, "Did you know your ID card is good on any service base?" Of course we know that now, but we didn't as wives new to the military.

Separated by Duty, United by Love: A Guide to Long-Distance Relationships for Military Couples, by Shellie Vandevoorde (2006). Comprehensive guide to how to prepare yourself for deployments, down to the gritty details of being prepared for the worst.

Surviving Deployment: A Guide for Military Families, by Karen M. Pavlicin (2003). Full of good examples and ideas for planning and preparing to survive deployment.

The Homefront Club: The Hardheaded Woman's Guide to Raising a Military Family, by Jacey Eckhart (2005). Often funny and very insightful guide to military life. We especially love her ideas on how to stay connected to extended family as you move.

That Military House: Move it, Organize it and Decorate it, by Sandee Payne (2006). Even though Kathie has moved nineteen times she immediately found new ideas to apply to her upcoming move!

Today's Military Wife: Meeting the Challenges of Service Life, by Lydia Sloan Cline is in its fifth edition (2003). A lot of good reference material as well as information on military customs and courtesies.

Under the Sabers; The Unwritten Code of Army Wives, by Tanya Biank (2006). Triggered by the Fort Bragg killings in 2002, this journalist, army daughter and new army spouse covers the experiences of Eighty-second Airborne spouses.

When Duty Calls: A Handbook for Families Facing Military Separation, by Carol Vandesteeg (2005). Another good book to read as you face a deployment, full of lessons learned by other families, resources available, and things to consider for yourself, your children, and your relationship.

While They're at War: The True Story of American Families on the Homefront, by Kristin Henderson (2006). We think all Americans should read this book so they would really understand the sacrifices they ask of our military and their families.

These books keep you from researching what has already been found, since the authors—all military spouses themselves—gathered tips and resources from military spouses and other experts.

Fiction Books—A Sampling

The Ocean Between Us, by Susan Wiggs (2004). When Kathie read this book, she thought immediately, "Susan has to be a military spouse—she captured how we feel." So we called her up to find out. She isn't (and wasn't) a military spouse, but interviewed enough of them in depth to write this authentic sounding novel about our lives.

The Yokota Officers Club, by Sarah Bird (2002). This will have you laughing and crying, and relating whether you were a military or civil service "brat" like the main character in the book, or simply someone who has experienced military life.

Many titles by marine spouse and romance writer Amy J. Fetzer have military life themes, such as *Tell It to the Marines, Perfect Weapon, Hit Hard, Naked Truth.* www.amyjfetzer.com.

Send us your favorite novels that have military lives at the core, and we'll add them to our website resources and to our next book. Email us at Kathie@militaryspousehelp.com or Holly@militaryspousehelp.com.

Magazines, Newspapers, and Newsletters

Your post/base newspaper is an important source of news about changes in military service benefits, in resources, and workshops available to you and in service information that might impact your spouse's career or assignment. Each of the services have an equivalent to the Associated Press service that provides important service-wide information that run as articles in your local post/base paper.

Air Force/Army/Marine Corps/Navy Times newspapers. Gannett publications. These are not published by the services, as some readers think. Their audience is military members, but they are useful publications for spouses to read as well. They give you a good understanding of what's happening around the military. Some articles each issue are geared to family members, especially those written by Karen Jowers (and our column called Married to the Military.)

Military.com's Department of Defense *Spouse/Family* Newsletter (includes our column on strategic career planning for military spouses)

Military Money magazine, from In Charge Publications. Check your commissary for free copies. NMFA members can request free copies be sent to their homes. www.militarymoney.com (includes our column on Mobile Careers, which are archived at militarymoney.com and on our website.)

Military Spouse magazine, the brainchild of two military spouses, available every two months in your exchange on base/post and in some Borders bookstores near large posts or by subscription from www.militaryspouse magazine.com (includes our Dare to Dream column where we help military spouses brainstorm ways to go for their dreams).

Service Resources

Every service has some great resources for military families and they keep improving. So be sure to ask what is available. Here is a list of all seven uniformed services of the United States. Did you know there were seven? We didn't either until we attended a National Military Family Association conference.

The Seven Uniformed Services of the United States official websites:

U.S. Air Force—www.af.mil/

U.S. Army—www.army.mil/

U.S. Coast Guard—www.uscg.mil/USCG.html

U.S. Marine Corps—www.usmc.mil/

U.S. Navy—www.navy.mil/

National Oceanic and Atmospheric Administration (NOAA), Officer
    Corps—www.noaacorps.noaa.gov/index.html

Commissioned Corps of the U.S. Public Health Service—www.usphs.gov/

As a basic, you can save yourself a lot of time and frustration as a new spouse by taking one of the Military 101–type programs available through each service. These programs provide you with a foundation of knowledge about this life and give you a chance to meet other spouses. You can take some of the classes online. We have found all the programs to be user friendly. They are not just for new spouses; even veteran spouses will be surprised at what they will learn. Check with your service's family center on post or base.

Air Force Heart Link

Army Family Team Building (AFTB)

Navy COMPASS

Marine Corps Family Team Building L.I.N.K.S. program

Websites

One note about websites. We chose not to attempt to include an exhaustive list of useful websites here. For one thing, there are so many. For another, many of them change too frequently to include. So we chose to include a few that are good gateways to further resources.

Military OneSource provides information and assistance in such areas as parenting and childcare, educational services, financial information and counseling, civilian legal advice, elder care, crisis support, and relocation information. We've mentioned this in some of the chapters but want to be sure everyone knows about it. Military OneSource is a great place to have your individual questions and concerns addressed, as well as a source to access free counseling services should you ever need them. www.militaryonesource.com (user ID: military; password: onesource).

National Military Family Association—www.nmfa.org.

We think every military spouse should be a member of the National Military Family Association, so you can keep up with and have input to testimony to Congress on issues concerning military families. Plus this is a great central source of information and resources that you can trust.

Operation Give a Hug—working to get Huggee Miss You Dolls into the hands of children dealing with deployment. www.operationgiveahug.org.

CINCHOUSE—www.cinchouse.com, the brainchild of Meredith Leyva —author of *Married to the Military*—and a joint effort of a group of military spouses, full of information and a great chat room to ask your questions and network with other spouses.

Military Homefront is an official Department of Defense website for reliable Quality of Life Information (and policy) designed to help troops and families, leaders, and service providers. www.militaryhomefront.dod.mil.

Index

About the Authors

PHOTO BY MARIANNE MARSHALL, ARMY SPOUSE AND OWNER OF PATTY-CAKE PHOTOGRAPHY

KATHIE HIGHTOWER and HOLLY SCHERER are military spouses. They co-author the Married to the Military column in the *Air Force/Army/Navy/Marine Corps Times* newspapers, the Dare to Dream column in *Military Spouse* magazine, a column on mobile careers in *Military Money* magazine and a column in Military.com's Department of Defense Spouse/Family newsletter.

Holly and Kathie have presented their trademark workshop Follow Your Dreams While You Follow the Military™ for military spouses since 1994 all over the United States, Europe, and Japan. Although they have partnered on writing and speaking projects since 1993, they have only lived in the same place one time for nine months. The rest of the work has been done virtually.

Kathie has spent most of her life connected to the military, from her entry into life as a civil service "brat" at age two in Berlin, Germany, to serving on first active duty, and then in the Army Reserves for more than twenty years, retiring as a Lieutenant Colonel, to being married to the military for twenty-eight years. She's worked at many different jobs during her nineteen moves as a military spouse, from staining furniture at a company in rural Alabama to corporate personnel manager to pharmaceutical sales representative to advertising sales representative to advertising agency account executive. Since 1989 she has had her own business doing speaking, writing, and conference coordinating for both military and civilian audiences. She currently lives in Tacoma, Washington, with her husband, Greg, and two cats, with future plans to move to the Oregon coast.

Holly has two master's degrees in early childhood special education and in human development and family relations. During her twenty-two years as a military spouse, she has worked as a child life specialist and educator at Johns Hopkins Hospital, as well as taught early childhood special education, worked as a caseworker for disabled adults, and prepared grants for nonprofit organizations and universities. She has a strong compassion for helping other military spouses and has been an active volunteer in each of the military communities where she has lived. She has received many awards for her volunteer work from the Volunteer of the Year, Commanding General's Soaring Eagle award, Heart of Victory award to Outstanding Civilian Service Medal and Commander's Award for Public Service. Holly lives in Memphis, Tennessee, with her husband, Jack, and twins, Helen and Jack.

AUSA Family Programs

The Association of the United States Army (AUSA) is another great resource for Military families. The Family Programs directorate works closely with the Army and private organizations on programs and initiatives which affect Army families including spouse employment and education opportunities among many others. They also offer free resource materials on a variety of topics upon request. Visit their website at www.ausa.org/family